From My Grandmother's Bedside

FROM MY GRANDMOTHER'S BEDSIDE

Sketches of Postwar Tokyo

Norma Field

. . .

University of California Press

Berkeley   Los Angeles   London

University of California Press
Berkeley and Los Angeles, California
University of California Press, Ltd.
London, England

Field, Norma, 1947-
    From my grandmother's bedside : sketches of
postwar Tokyo / Norma Field.
        p.   cm.
    Includes bibliographical references.
    ISBN 0-520-20844-7 (alk. paper)
    1. Japan—Social life and customs—1945–   .
    I. Title.
D5822.5.F54   1997
952.04—dc21   97-18526

Printed in the United States of America
9 8 7 6 5 4 3 2 1
The paper used in this publication meets the
minimum requirements of American National
Standard for Information Sciences—
Permanence of Paper for Printed Library
Materials, ANSI Z39.48-1984.

For Lucian Marquis
and
Ishigaki Rin

WALKING-STICK PASS
Ishigaki Rin

I called on distant relatives
near Lake Suwa in Shinshū.

The old woman I was seeing after a long absence
had taken ill, grown speechless
and was resting quietly.

Showing the undulation of the years
of raising eight children,
the small ridge ended there
where, from the hollow of a round rump,
she dropped a form steaming with life.

When I climbed the height known as Walking-stick Pass,
the entire Yatsugatake Range opened up before my eyes
    snow-draped mountains
    resting in the distance.

Somehow my hand was sure of the chill
of the white under-robe brought by winter,
of the warmth of flesh just showing at the collar.
The bare trees like downy fuzz,
the clouds billowing from the valleys.

I had been made to stand in a place like a lookout
with a view of two instances of nature.
Under the clear sky
I held my nose and endured
that which was large and beautiful.

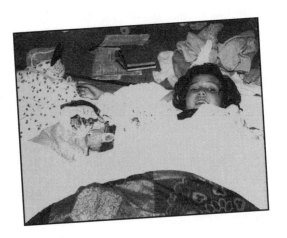

Clutter Love

My father's Polaroid camera was an object of scorn and wonder among the family. One day in May, over forty years ago, he used it to shoot this picture of his daughter during one of those periods of preventive detention following a bout of cold or (at worst) a touch of bronchitis, when the household was mobilized in order to keep a robust child in bed. For my mother and grandmother, the possibility that somewhere, in some single cell, a virus still lurked—or that a new one, predicted by meteorological signs, hovered on the horizon—justified the deferral yet again of the day for my "getting up." My unmarried aunts brought home books and toys, while my mother and grandmother exercised all their ingenuity to keep me warm, even in late spring (note the sweater button that peeks from under my flannel nightgown). My mother sat at my pillow to keep me company, making up stories or reading out loud. Now and then, I grudgingly allowed her breaks, during which she would skim the newspaper. Some rules, however, had to be loosened to accommodate this extended confinement. Thus I was allowed to have Mimi, the family cat, near me, sometimes even in bed (the threat of fleas presumably deemed preferable to that of viruses), and Mimi allowed herself to be dressed in my baby clothes. The doll, also bundled up, had been a birthday present from my grandmother a year or two earlier. Crushed that she was not a fancy American doll with flesh-colored rubber limbs, blond curls, and eyes that opened and shut, I also couldn't bear to let my grandmother see my disappointment. So, willing her to be my favorite, I played with her and came to love her.

. . .

PREFACE

We rarely see sorrowful dockside partings any more, observes the poet Ishigaki Rin. She is commenting on a poem in which the speaker recalls a scene from boyhood: his family huddled together at a northern port for a long farewell, waiting for a steamboat to take his grandparents away. His grandfather presses a coin into his hand. His father whispers to his grandfather, then tells him to give the coin back. Both men have tears in their eyes. The poem ends in the present, sixty years later:

> Sleeping quietly Grandfather Grandmother Father Mother—
> I am also grown old.

The poem is "Steamboat," by Tanaka Fuyuji (1894–1980). Ishigaki could have included train stations and especially airports as places for good-byes that are now mostly light-hearted—insofar as people see each other off at all, that is. What disappeared from our world along with sad farewells?

I know the question invites nostalgia, which I cannot scorn, but it can't be absorbed by it. Some of the answers are strewn along the passage, never complete, from a world of suffering

Preface

to one of stress. It's that passage I try to explore in the writing that follows, writing prompted by a stay in Tokyo in the summer of 1995, the season for observing the fiftieth anniversary of the end of the War. I want to draw together the parts of the history we live more and more disjunctively. With what effect, I can't now know, though some yokings may be jarring, too idiosyncratic, even, to seem persuasive.

But I hope this book isn't only a willful collection of fragments, not least because of the friends, acquaintances, and strangers who extended insights, gestures, anecdotes, sustenance. Here I want to thank just a few of them: Kozaki Setsuko, Zhang Zhen, Igarashi Akio, Diana Young, Uezato Kazumi, Mariko Tamanoi, Kawazoe Fusae, Candace Vogler, Hiyane Miyoko, Kathy Rupp, Kondaibō Mie, and Tsushima Chitose. Leora Auslander has been that vital thing, a comrade in mulling. Bill Sibley continues to prompt me to relish the experience of the day for itself. Earl Miner gave me the pleasure of back-and-forthing on poetry translation. I also want to thank those who have over the years helped me on chases, unsuccessful as well as successful, after stray bits of information: Eizaburo Okuizumi and Kuki Yoko of the East Asia Library at the University of Chicago, Ichiko Morita of the Japan Documentation Center at the Library of Congress, and Amanda Seaman. I am grateful to Marilyn Young and Anne Allison for their generosity in reading the manuscript for the University of California Press; Anne helped me to see it from outside my own head, and Marilyn pushed me on details from her own catholic knowledge and engagement with history. I thank Sheila Levine for being willing to tackle this experiment.

Laura Driussi and Dore Brown make professionalism attractive. I am soberly but gratefully indebted to Evan Camfield, copyeditor and therefore reader extraordinaire.

Lucian Marquis took me on as a student when I came back to mundane college life in 1968 after a junior year in France. That was a thrilling time to be alive in many places around the world, and I came back exhilarated and impatient. Lucian prodded me to think about what had happened with some discipline and showed me how. That is to say, he showed me how one comes to have ideas at all. His academic subject was politics, but it was always made legible in juxtaposition with literature, history, music, sociology. Indeed, I can't think of anything that would be irrelevant for Lucian Marquis, in whom living and learning are inseparable from each other. I thank him for his example and for continuing to be my teacher.

I have a special debt to Ishigaki Rin, whose poem I translate at the beginning. Ishigaki was born in 1920 in Tokyo. After completing what was then called "higher elementary school" at age fourteen, she went to work for a bank, not because she necessarily had to but because she wanted to have her own time and money for writing and subscribing to poetry journals. She ended up working at that bank for some forty years until she retired.

Her first poems to become well known were written during the heyday of postwar union activism. Often, her poetry dwells on the details of everyday life. For such reasons she has been called a "bank clerk poet" and especially, a poet of "life." The Japanese word is *seikatsu*, which marks "life" with the accent of "livelihood." Ishigaki herself, writing about the common linkage of her poems to "life," muses over how this word smells of poverty while "art" is somehow luxurious. It's important to distinguish between objecting to the spirit behind such labels and objecting to the labels themselves. Rejecting the labels not only accedes tacitly to the judgment that writing close to work or everyday life is necessarily impoverished but simultaneously contributes to the illusion that the works of poets not so labeled in fact float free, unrelated to the world of labor and everyday life, in the stratosphere of—existence?

When asked her aspirations for poetry, Ishigaki says, she can never come up with a proper answer: "It is not that I have special hopes for poetry, but that my wishes and prayers for real life are intertwined with poetry and inextricable from it. So at times I have answered, 'How wonderful it would be if the poems I have ended up writing were to be useful.'" Elsewhere, thinking about the impact of literary prizes on her life, Ishigaki notes how increased attention and demand for her work resulted in the utter neglect of her personal ties. It is then that she achieves this clarity: "I had been hoping that the scab called 'life' would peel off naturally from my poetry. But when I thought about what could be born from a way of life careless of human connection, I began to have a strange worry. If life were to peel off from the poetry of life, it would end up just plain poetry!"

During the period when I was working on this book, I often traveled with Ishigaki's poems and essays. They made life instantly less lonely. The also introduced me to many contemporary Japanese poems that I would have been sorry to miss.

Preface

My own familiarity with Japanese poetry had been largely confined to premodern, fixed-form verse. Ishigaki's poems gave me
that rare thing after youth, a new hunger. It made me fall in
love with the language all over again, or rather, as if for the
first time.

All translations in the text that follows are my own. Japanese
names appear in standard order, surname first. A version of
"The Anniversary of a Lie" appeared as "The Devastating
Absence of Surprise" in *The Bulletin of Concerned Asian Scholars* 27,
no. 3 (1995), 18–19, and is here reprinted with the kind permission of the editors.

JEWELED DREAM

My grandmother is my mother's jewel.

The words form in my predawn sleep. *Jewel, treasure,* I can't tell if the words are coming in English or Japanese. But I awake to the thought, It's all right, then.

My grandmother is my mother's jewel.

It's all right. I can go home again.

CALIFORNIA WINE

Twenty years after its opening, the Tokyo International Airport at Narita continues to be called the New Narita Tokyo International Airport in the English announcements issuing from the limo speaker. The voice is synthetic female, the accent a regionless, classless simulation of British English. From the seats behind mine, an indeterminate number of male American voices fill the air during the ride into the city, normally requiring ninety minutes, but on this Saturday evening, under heavy monsoon skies, stretching to two hours.

—Where're we going, anyway?

— Dunno. Here, let me take a look at this map. Well, we're not too far from Tokyo Station.

— D'you know where to go tonight?

—Yeah, we're going to Roppongi. The main drag. I know a great place to eat. It's really spectacular. You won't believe it.

—Do they cook things there?

—Yeah. I don't like Japanese food.

—Aren't you gonna prepare for the meeting tomorrow?

—If I can find the papers.

—You're gonna wing it? . . . Where're we going next?

—Singapore. No. Malaysia. Then Thailand.

—Do they have business class out there?

—Yeah, they've got it out of somewhere. Where was it. Fukien.

—They've got business class out of Fukien?

—Yeah, Fukien.

A long silence. I wonder if they're dozing off, as I am. Flights from New York, Chicago, and Seattle arrived within minutes of each other. Wherever they're from, they've been traveling for a while. One of them begins reading out loud.

—"Welcome to Japan. During June we have a rainy season. Yesterday it rained, today it is raining, tomorrow it will rain, Sunday will be fine."

Laughter.

—"Maybe you will have jet lag. So tomorrow, I will meet you at hotel around 9:30 or 10:00."

Guffaws.

—"I will call you from hotel front. As you well know, my English is not so good. Please speak slowly. Yours. . . ." How d'you pronounce his name?

—How's it spelled?

—S-h-i-n-i-c-h-i.

—In the Army we'd say, Hey, Alphabet Soup, get over here.

—No, no, no. "Shin'ichi."

This is the voice that identified Fukien. It's the same one that knew the great restaurant in Roppongi. The pronunciation is powerfully American but plausible. Pity for Shin'ichi wells up from the depths of my jet lag. These men don't know, don't care to know, how carefully he's planned their visit, how early he'll get up in order to meet them at 9:30 or 10:00. I become indignant on Shin'ichi's behalf, then check myself. This is the new Japan. It's probably Shin'ichi who has the advantage.

If so, these Americans are happily unaware. They aren't young. One of them has already referred to a son's graduation. They talk about faxes and voice mail matter-of-factly. Small-scale multinational entrepreneurs? Maybe Army experience allows one of them to call himself a Far East expert.

Conversation starts up again between the two seated directly behind me. Because they are no longer trying to communicate across the aisle, their voices are muted. Even so, the entire bus seems poised on their words.

—I'm glad Clinton's doing what he's doing.

—So am I. There oughta be a lot more American cars on this road.

—Wonder why he's just going after the luxury cars, though. He oughta go after all of them.

—He's gotta start somewhere.

The urge to retort grips my throat: What about the World Trade Organization? Don't you know cars aren't really the problem? Show me one thing NAFTA's done for American workers, anyway. But my brain hears a tired voice, female and pedagogical, and the impulse subsides. I don't feel like disrupting their camaraderie, secure in the presumption of being unheard, or rather, uncomprehended. I'm glad I can't see them. They don't see me. At most, they see the top of my head, as disembodied as their voices. These limousine buses come with luxuriously high-backed seats.

Even the static monsoon sky darkens as the bus hums along the expressway, punctuated only by electronic boards announcing the length of various stretches of congestion. Silence settles on the bus.

—What's that you got there?

—I saved the wine from dinner.

—Why'd you do that?

—Hey, I've got an idea. This is what we'll give'm. Alphabet Soup. What'd you say his name was?

—Shin'ichi?

—Very nice. Very, very nice. California wine. I saved mine, too. We'll tell him this is the real thing, California wine.

Another challenge for Shin'ichi. He will have to produce surprised gratitude for wine he would find tossed in the bins of his local supermarket, selling for the equivalent of a very few dollars.

The party gets out at the first hotel stop. There are five or six of them, mostly middle-aged, dressed inconspicuously enough. There's nothing about them to offend the casual glance.

The bus heaves a collective sigh and stretches its limbs to fill the space left by the Americans. Here and there, muffled conversation rises into the dark.

From My Grandmother's Bedside

ESCALATOR CONFUSION

Only a few hours earlier, I wouldn't have thought to identify with Shin'ichi. The plummeting dollar of the preceding few months had precipitated the phrase "currency exile" as my likely fate, and stepping into Narita I found myself wearing it as a secret badge of martyrdom. Lacking a yen income, how much longer would I be able to keep coming home?

It's still early for the touristic migrations of summer. Alone on the escalator leading to immigration and customs, I am veiled in anticipatory mourning. A certain loftiness, even romance, inheres in the word *exile*, but there's an unglamorous aspect to my alienation. It's the whiff of poverty. No, I prefer to think of it as austerity. Approaching the gleaming floors and orderly space, I brace myself.

Prosperous middle-classness is the postwar Japanese national identity. The hard years after surrender have congealed as fable, and even the malaise now setting in after the bursting of the bubble economy only confirms the degree to which prosperity had become the norm. Slipping from that middle-class identity threatens my precarious national filiation. My Occupation soldier-father met and married my Japanese mother a year before I was born, giving me American citizenship long before I would set foot in the United States. I was never a Japanese citizen, for until 1985, Japanese citizenship could not be granted through the mother. American citizenship regulations governing citizens born abroad had a residency requirement (eventually struck down as discriminatory), so for a while I ran the risk of ending up stateless. By now, quite apart from my legal status, my clothing, gestures, and even features are stamped American. Does that mean people will think of me as a more mature, sedate version (marked, therefore, with pathos?) of the young white men and women who spread their generic ethnic jewelry outside the National Museum of Western Art?

I'm getting carried away. Even I can see that. Maybe it's just a version of the hysteria induced by transpacific crossings, probably by any adult homecoming.

In the limo my heart went out to Shin'ichi because the confident American male voices threw me back to a childhood when all Japanese, men and women, looked small and poor and Americans tall and strong. In any case, it's entirely possible for Shin'ichi to be the entrepreneurial gopher for the Roppongi-dining Americans in the new global economy. And there remains the fact that they speak better English, and that their ignorance of Japanese doesn't count. I may be stunningly wrong, but I still think they're likely to be taller, too.

I'm taken aback by how much I'm afraid of being—of seeming—poor, ever so mildly and even temporarily. Back in Chicago, I'd be instantly, unmistakably, middle class. So how is this different from, say, the (hoped-for) passing poverty of young-adult studenthood? And do I believe that being middle class constitutes my authentic self, which I'm pained to have misrecognized? Is it that the sensation of schooling, profession, and an assortment of social competencies melting away along with a dissolving dollar makes me queasy?

As a child, I think I understood citizenship as permission to stay in a certain place. I was fearful of being snatched away from home. Now I can see that so much of the way class is lived has to do with where you feel you have a right to be, or where you feel you belong, because you can easily feel yourself an impostor even when you have not only the right but the means to be someplace. And where you can go and where you can stay are hugely important in determining your identity. No wonder a threat to class identity can feel like a threat to national identity, and vice versa.

The home I dreaded being taken from was my grandparents' small house and garden, but I also knew, without understanding how, that they were part of an entity called "Japan." I didn't want to be taken from Japan, but in the public world of school bus and playground, although I identified *with* puny Japanese against gigantic Americans, I didn't want to be identified *as* Japanese. I suppose I could rationalize and say that I intuited that my right to stay in Japan depended on possession of what was then an awkwardly sized gray booklet, a United States passport. But I think I simply and cravenly preferred to be identified with power.

At passport renewal time I stood dumb in a cavernous room in the embassy, smelling the American smell of disinfectant. America was the land where germs couldn't survive, I thought. (Japan, by contrast, swarmed with deadly germs. My father had impressed me with an encyclopedia picture of a horse's cadaver to reinforce his warning not to eat Japanese strawberries.) My right hand was raised too high, as if I were back in the classroom where, scanning my modest collection of English words, I would force myself to participate, to keep up the show of belonging with teachers, classmates, and most of all myself. The embassy official muttered the oath and a long silence followed, my weary arm still raised Statue-of-Liberty fashion, until my mother whispered, Yes, and I said, fervently, thankfully, Yes. If the grown man felt silly asking a child in a starched cotton dress whether she would refrain from aiding or giving comfort to the enemies of the United States, he didn't let on.

In my childhood in early postwar Japan, citizenship as confident propriety, easy laughter, and imposing stride—as the right to be there—was American. Overwhelmingly, it was also male. Had I sniffed harder through the air of disinfected authority, I might have sorted out the smell of my father's masculinity—sour, inconsequential, yet menacing.

Now that, as people tirelessly repeat, the cold war is history, I mostly cluck my tongue over the spectacle of American embassy staff administering loyalty oaths to children. I have even begun to imagine with sympathy the lives of all those American boys who came home from the War with exotic brides, the boys who came back to uncomprehending if not hostile families, who awoke on American shores to the silent immobility of non-English-speaking, non-driving women.

Nevertheless, it felt good to be inconspicuous in the dark limo, to fancy myself joining in the collective relief of the Japanese passengers when the Americans got off.

HOMECOMING

—I'm home, Obaachama. It's me.

My grandmother's eyes roll up. I am afraid. I've seen this twice before when she lost consciousness. Both times, she came back to the world in a flood of perspiration. This time I can see that she's breathing. So I can breathe too. Stop, I want to say to the pupils. Stop and hold me. I'll stay still. Does that make it easier? Just hold on to my face and let me into your mind.

—I came back to see you. I promised I would. Last summer. Remember?

Her pupils have stopped drifting. We lock onto each other's gaze.

—Can you tell who I am?

Her lips are closed tight, making her jaw square.

—Can you tell who I am?

Gravely, almost imperceptibly, she shakes her head, No. The next morning, she will nod, Yes. Equally gravely, equally faintly.

I need to learn to read these signs. It's imprecise to talk about nods, a careless surrender to habit. It's not that her head moves to signal the difference between yes and no. Maybe her jaw muscles shift. Maybe it's a flicker of the eyelid. But her meaning is unmistakable.

More than twenty years ago, a teacher said his body had learned to register minute temperature changes in Hawai'i. He wanted to show how one might become a reader of ninth-century Japanese poetry, to develop the capacity to appreciate faint variations between two assemblies of thirty-one syllables dedicated to, say, late spring snow. Some years later, I understood what he meant while waiting for the subway in lower Manhattan. It was July, I was enormously pregnant, and succeeding waves of friends needed to be shown around New York. The fleeting movement of air inside the black tunnel before and after the passage of a train made it a source of refreshment more munificent than a roaring window air conditioner.

Now, three years after her first stroke and two months after the second, I experience again the force of minute difference in peering at my grandmother's face. I don't know if I will learn to read its signals.

FANS

The kitchen fan died today.

It was at least twenty years old, but even so it was incomparably more advanced than American fans today. To call it a thing of grace would be excessive, but its blades were a translucent azure, its neck telescoped with the flick of a lever, its arc adjusted from 180 degrees to zero. The wider the angle, of course, the greater number of people who could benefit from its fleeting breeze. That was how my grandmother preferred it, even when she was standing over a wok frying shrimp and vegetables in August. She didn't like too much air coming at her, whether from a train or bus window (in the days before such vehicles were uniformly air conditioned) or from a fan. It wasn't good for her weak heart, she would say. It was the closest she came to complaining. Like many Japanese—it must have been a conspicuous news item years ago—she believed that letting the fan blow on you all night was an invitation to disaster. She predicted it would lead to death from heart failure. (Seeing me emerge for breakfast morning after morning never dislodged that conviction.) At any rate, Japanese fans, including the one that died, come with timers. In addition to the numbered settings for degrees of strength, the kitchen fan had one labeled "Refreshing." It was weaker than the weakest, number three; it was my grandmother's favorite, and its button was larger than the others and colored to match the blades. She showed alarm if she found that someone had (mistakenly, she was sure) pressed the number two button. This was a fan made for her.

When my children were small, all the fans in the house—the kitchen fan, the upstairs fan, the downstairs fan for guests—were covered with lace trimmed with elastic for a snug fit. In retrospect it seems unlikely that these pretty covers would have kept a determined toddler's fingers from the blades, but such exploration in fact never took place. Was it because the delicate netting in aquamarine or pale green (*refreshing* colors) sufficiently signified "barrier"? By contrast, the real barriers, the sliding doors in my grandmother's house, whether of translucent white paper for separating rooms from verandahs or heavy patterned paper for separating closets from rooms or rooms from each other, were riddled with holes created by the fingers of my children and generations of cousins. My grandmother was never annoyed, even when a crib had been foolishly placed next to a newly repapered door.

At the end of the summer, my grandmother cleaned the fans and shrouded their awkward forms before putting them to rest, just as she drained, cleaned, and wrapped up the kerosene stoves each spring. In later years these became my mother's annual tasks. Since her stroke, my grandmother has lain in a room whose temperature is regulated by a computerized heater/air conditioner installed near the ceiling of the room next to hers. (It was still unthinkable to have cold or hot air blowing directly on her.) Whenever she thinks of it, which is often, my mother stoops to read the thermostat on the remote control placed on my grandmother's nightstand. Inevitably, she is moved to grasp it, march to the next room, and aim it at the sleek grey god. To the accompaniment of discreet beeps, its green eyes blink; flaps open and close. As if this weren't enough, a hygrometer has appeared on the wall next to the nightstand. Now my mother studies this instrument more religiously than the thermostat. Predictably, she gasps at the reading and invokes the Summer Dry setting. Why can't you rely on your own body, I grumble. Japan is different, she says, not bothering to be defensive. You don't know how humid it gets here. How has she managed to make it absurd for me to point out that I was born here, that I have spent nearly half my life here and most pertinently, virtually every summer?

The kitchen fan is sitting outside by the gate now, waiting for the Large-sized Trash Pickup requested by my mother. I bring the upstairs fan down to take its place. It's almost as old as the dead fan but much less used. I wash its blades and frame with vinegar, the kind sold as "salad" vinegar in American supermarkets, a cut above generic vinegar. It's not as rusty as the old kitchen fan. My mother turns it on with excessive alacrity for these dark monsoon days. I find that I have to change seats. I miss the Refreshing setting.

TIME

A week has passed since the limo ride. I run along a route plotted to take me by favorite houses that no longer stand while avoiding others whose reasons for avoidance are mostly forgotten. Every step restores my equilibrium, adjusts my limbs, eyes, ears, and even tongue to the territory. Idly I think, what about the twelve hours lost over the International Date Line? Of course, they're made up when I cross the other way. What if I never did, though? Is that day lost forever? I know the twenty-four time zones are arbitrary demarcations. Human lines laid over the face of the globe. But they are also tied to the time of the solar system. If I never recross the date line, the hours lost to me are lived cumulatively westward, until, finally, they spill over the Greenwich meridian and become a twelve-hour day.

We move through twenty-four hours apiece three hundred sixty-five times a year. Alternatively, at any given hour, we collectively make up the length of the sun's shadow across the earth.

NEIGHBORHOOD I

On a Sunday morning around seven o'clock, no one is stirring. For some years, probably three decades, all the streets in my grandmother's neighborhood have been paved. Last summer's record-breaking heat was made the more unbearable by the unabsorbing asphalt. Ishigaki Rin, on the verge of old age, writes about how it's no longer possible to wear clogs because they're too noisy on paved streets. But it was precisely that clatter I once loved: the music of the street, from a brief moment when wooden clogs and asphalt came together.

Grand or modest, all the streets are cramped. Garage doors line the more aspiring ones. Side by side they are blank eyes turned upon the silent morning. Soon they will open their heavy lids. Out come—not cartoon flames, but gleaming cars, aloof to the narrowness of the street. Their drivers are fiercely skilled: day in and day out, they execute egress and entry without sound or scratch.

FLOWER TALK

A burst of astonishing blue stopped me in my tracks as I walked absent-mindedly to the neighborhood library to copy articles from month-old newspapers. It was a hydrangea bush, tall enough to fall into that ambiguous zone between bush and tree. When I was little, I was entranced by hydrangea blue, and I begged and begged my grandmother to get one of our very own for the garden. She said the bushes grew too big. Eventually she broke down, but by then my heart was unavailable for capture by a magical shade of blue.

Hydrangea changes color from blue to purple to pink or crimson in the course of a flowering season. Therefore, says my pocket dictionary, it symbolizes fickleness. The usage example has it modifying *woman.*

This one on the street was of the variety called "picture frame," in which each bloom consists of what look like fully opened blossoms encircling tightly closed buds. Five days later I passed the street-corner bush, then turned back sharply. Where there had been hundreds, not a single blossom remained. The stems were cut clean, their white edges raw against the dark green leaves. Evidently no fickleness is permitted in this household.

From My Grandmother's Bedside

My aunt next door brings over potted flowers for the garden and arrangements for the house nearly every day. A woman of abundant talent, she seems not to know how, or lacks the patience, to grow flowers herself, or to make them bloom from year to year. When my grandmother was healthy, this youngest daughter brought all her ailing pots for her mother to cure. Now she fills the garden with purchased pots. The arrangements for the house combine all manner of flowers, usually pink, one of my aunt's favorite colors. Along with flowers, she skewers multicolored paper birds into a sponge base. She replenishes the water in the plastic container every day. Because the whole affair is done up in lacy cellophane and ribbons, she cannot tell how much water to add. Later, my mother removes the soaked doily underneath. If she doesn't catch it, the Home Helper will, with much muttering. The Helper has been coming mornings since my grandmother came home from the hospital four years ago. She is a force to be reckoned with, as such personages are apt to become.

My aunt has also tried planting some of the potted plants in the ground. After nightfall, my mother pulls each stem from the ground. My other aunt, the middle sister, once threw all the flower pots purchased by her younger sister into the street. (Good thing no one was passing by, is my mother's afterthought.)

A potted picture-frame hydrangea sits outside the front door. It has already changed color twice. My mother says she will toss this pot the day after tomorrow, a Combustible Trash Pickup day.

All three sisters like flowers, the middle one passionately. The garden was my grandmother's great luxury. Her flowering trees and her perennials were also the delight of passersby. Would she have dreamed that flowers would become weapons in her daughters' hands?

In the meantime, a city in the metropolitan region has begun a "sunflowers for peace" campaign. Sunflower seedlings are being handed out at local schools on successive Sundays. In the spring schoolchildren had started thousands of plants from seed. The idea is that on August 15, the anniversary of surrender, full-grown sunflowers will impress the bright face of peace upon the citizenry.

Following Jacques Chirac's announcement of the resumption of nuclear testing in the South Pacific, Australian labor has called for a boycott of French goods. In the Only Country in the World to be Hit by Atomic Bombs, no one is clamoring for a boycott.

Sunflowers forever.

BEDDING

It is also possible to wage wars over bedding.

—Isn't it a little chilly for her?

—I don't think so.

—It feels chilly to me.

—In fact her forehead was a little sweaty, so I just now took her hands out from under the covers.

—I think we need something in between the summer terry cloth and the springweight comforter.

—Where am I supposed to store everything you buy?

From My Grandmother's Bedside

My mother's voice is turning yellow, according to the Japanese expression. But that will not deter my aunt, on the other end of the phone line. In my pragmatic mode I say, Let her buy whatever she wants. Let her cover Obaachama however she wants. We can take it off as soon as she leaves.

—But I don't know where to put the stuff she brings over.

By now my mother's voice is thinning into a wail. Throw it out then, I say. But bedding is bulky. Will she have to request a Large-sized Trash Pickup?

Soon a new comforter arrives, exactly the weight of the spring-fall one my mother has been using. My aunt clucks with satisfaction as she drapes it over her mother's body. As soon as she is home, however, she calls the Home Helper to ask whether she shouldn't have bought a longer one. The Home Helper has become expert in the art of conversation as practiced by my family. Soothingly, she intones, Don't forget, there's always next year. The next day, however, a longer version of the flowery comforter arrives.

The monsoon this year has been cooler than I remember, and I nestle luxuriously under the summerweight comforter my grandmother bought when I first came home married. Its filling is all cotton, a rarity today except in bedding for babies, who must have the purest. For years I haven't quite seen the lovely top fabric because bedding is obsessively covered here, though often with translucent tops to let the design show tantalizingly through. I wonder where the covers to this set have disappeared to. The household rules pertaining to seasonal laundry and exchange have fallen by the wayside since the stroke.

Every few years, when I was little, my grandmother took apart the household bedding (something like, but not quite,

the futons sold in America today) and sent out the cotton filling to be "rebeaten." Sure enough, the darkened damp clumps
of cotton would be reborn white and fluffy, wrapped in
plump, neat packages. Then a day for refilling would be set
aside. My grandmother would shut the sliding doors to the
largest room in the house, cover her head with a dish towel,
and get to work. I was never allowed to watch, on what
grounds I'm not sure, but probably something about how
breathing the cotton would surely set me coughing. But of
course I peeked, and therefore I remember those days as days
of combat between my grandmother and the flying cotton.

For a few days, possibly a week, the redone bedding was the
height of luxury. That sense could be recaptured during the
spring, autumn, and winter on those days when there was
space in the garden to spread the bottom futon out in the sun.
(The garden was often occupied by laundry and, for a time,
the postcard-sized photographs of movie stars that my grandparents made for a living. Now there are electric futon dryers
for those who work during the day, those who have no space
for putting out their bedding, or for anybody during rainy
spells. It's an example of the Japanese domestic appliance rev-
olution, though one presumably without export value.) It's still
possible to hear in parts of Tokyo around three in the afternoon the sound of bedding being beaten free of dust before
being taken into the house. At night, burrowing into the co-
coon charged with energy absorbed from the sun, even the pale
winter sun, it never occurred to me to want an electric blanket.
Getting into bed on those nights when the bedding had not
been put out was another matter. I devised exercises to abbre-

viate contact with frigid sheets, exercises so frenzied that once I strained my neck and had to spend a day and a half with my head turned at right angles to my body, an experience that revitalized the metaphor of "facing." The varieties of fleecy winter sheets now available, combined with improved heating, have rendered superfluous both juvenile frenzy and stoic forbearance.

And on a midsummer night, what can surpass the scratchy pleasure of the classic, stiffly starched, waffle-patterned sheet?

Do most societies fetishize bedding? If so, which aspects? Would that make a respectable anthropological project, a global study of bedding? I think of the outpour of color from the interior furnishings pages of the mail-order catalogues that have become a staple of household mail in the U.S. The madly lavish boudoirs depicted therein are neither enticing nor reposeful. How can the American bourgeoisie expect to repair its damaged daylight life in those frenzied settings?

Evidently, it isn't just idiosyncrasy that turned bedding into such a charged topic in my family. The need for sleep is unrecognized by most children. I understood the principal purpose of lying prone as recovery from or—more important—prevention of illness. Bed therefore became a site of surveillance. Endlessly confined with colds, I was subject to unannounced inspections to confirm that my arms and shoulders were not visible above the comforter. That meant I had to read on my stomach, with only my head sticking out, turtle-fashion. During summer naps I tried to hold every muscle still under the terry-cloth blanket as my mother stood at the threshold, poised to pounce at the first sign of wakefulness. That was when she was convinced that without an hour's nap each day I was bound to contract encephalitis. To fall asleep at one o'clock each afternoon was no easy task for a child with a seven o'clock bedtime, quite apart from the magically contrary power of the command to sleep. Did my mother want to confirm my healthful slumber, or was she secretly unsatisfied on those rare occasions when she failed to detect a flickering eyelid?

Now, the hint of a cough from my grandmother summons my mother to her bedside "in a flash," as the English cliché goes, day or night. They have not been apart for more than a year since my mother was born. Until my grandmother's stroke they slept side by side. For the past three years, not counting hospital stays, they have been separated by six feet of floor and three feet of elevation, since my grandmother lies on a mechanized German hospital bed rented from a municipal agency. It comes with an air mattress whose waves are maintained at the desired level of firmness by an electric pump. The bed's multiple settings allow my grandmother to lie low enough for even my mother, four foot ten in full adulthood and shrinking with the combined effects of age and osteoporosis, to care for her with relative ease.

My grandmother, who gave birth to my mother, the eldest child, at the age of nineteen, spent a good deal of her young maternity keeping her three girls in bed. Besides persuading a neighborhood doctor to make frequent house calls, that meant carrying trays of food and bedpans, running inhalers, applying mustard plasters, and most of all staying up nights and worrying. Was this but the expression of neurotic personality? To a degree. My great-grandmother was evidently an enlightened person and a modern housewife, exceptionally informed about hygiene and nutrition. No less vigilant, her daughter, my grandmother, could not ward off all the microbes seeking to penetrate her young daughters' bodies. There were many things she did not let them eat—popsicles, bananas, cotton candy and other street fair treats—and she kept them indoors and preferably in bed at the first sneeze. But the water that was available was well water, and she kept house with six young male live-in employees for the movie-star photography business. One cough and the entire household was liable to come down sick. The cramped house was all the more airless for the commanding allocation of space to a darkroom. In the days before vaccination and sulfa drugs, classrooms were commonly dotted with empty desks whose occupants had contracted tuberculosis. My grandmother had seen her own classmates disappear that way, and she had seen other people's children die of dysentery. Her girls were the fragile redemption of a marriage that had been instantly and brutally unhappy. She kept them in bed in the hope of keeping them at all.

Such habits reappeared in the difficult postwar years when I was born. My mother reminds me of how my grandmother buried her head under the covers in order to change my diapers without exposing me to the chill air.

Bedding, in my family history, is the stuff of anxious mother love.

THE NEWS

There is so much news here. Day and night, events unfolding in a tiny village in the archipelago, events from the furthest reaches of the globe, and of course non-events in world cities turn into news, flooding our homes with sound waves, screen images, and newsprint.

Aung San Suu Kyi was released. The Japanese media immediately obtain interviews with people close to her, packaging their joy for a public habituated to a cynical politics. It works; it moves. And therefore alienates. Most viewers, safe, bored, and tired, would be hard put to imagine a comparable experience of political commitment, pain, and rejoicing—of sheer meaning. Commentators note that the military leaders of Myanmar, as they steadfastly call this nation, hope that with this measure they will silence the human-rights criticisms of Euroamerican countries. There is ambiguity in this morsel of information. Does it imply that we (Japanese) have had no human-rights objections to the Myanmar regime? That human rights are a Western notion imposed on "us," though we are too advanced to say that? But we've never been too sure whether we want to identify with Asia anyway. No question we're bursting with pride over Hideo Nomo, though, and hope he's going to break the strikeout record in the American All-Star game. (That's got a lot to do with his being Japanese, which still has something to do with being non-white, and that probably has something to do with being Asian.) So we might as well feel good about Ms. Suu Kyi's release and not worry too much about what it means for us.

No doubt there are newscasters who are chagrined at having to report on the activity of *Rainbow Warrior II*, sent by Greenpeace to the South Pacific, and the Australian and New Zealand protests against the resumption of French nuclear testing. Why are we so restrained given that we, after all, are the Only Country in the World to be Hit by Atomic Bombs?

Then there is the business of business. Europeans and Americans care about that, too. Japan is slightly tardy in exploiting opportunities in Burma, the U.S. very much so in Vietnam—virgin lands in the hottest economic region of the world today.

Another business loop: Japan has some of its used nuclear reactor fuel reprocessed in the U.K. and in France. In late 1992, a Japanese vessel loaded with one and a half tons of recovered plutonium set sail from Cherbourg, but some countries refused to allow the ship to pass through territorial waters. Consequently, the ship followed a route on the scale of sixteenth-century voyages of exploration, around the Cape of Good Hope through the Tasman Sea to Ibaragi Prefecture, just north of Tokyo.

One hundred A-bomb victims and their families sit in silent protest at the Hiroshima Peace Park. Aoshima Yukio, a former comedian who is now governor of Tokyo, meets with Jacques Chirac on his tour to apologize for cancelling the Tokyo expo, a decision of stunning financial, social, and environmental good sense. Chirac's previous job as mayor of Paris should have taught him a thing or two about the headaches of running a world city. Aoshima wants to slip in a "By the way, Jacques, won't you reconsider that decision in the South Pacific?" The president of France can understand why the governor of Tokyo would object to nuclear testing, but there are to be only seven or eight blasts, no damage at all to the environment.

Then let him do it in Paris, says my mother.

NEIGHBORHOOD II

I am reminded that my grandmother had a rule of thumb when judging people by their houses. It had to do with the size of the house in proportion to the lot. Well, "judging" is more my notion than hers. She would simply say, ruefully, I wouldn't want such a big house. Then she might add, I'd want more room for a garden.

Almost all the new houses in the neighborhood—no, *all* (sometimes it's better to throw qualificatory caution to the winds)—strain against their boundaries, and therefore against each other. A nondescript bush or two near the entrance becomes a sign of decency, or perhaps of pretentious excess. Most structures are blithely, candidly, denuded.

Living now in the American midwest, I have no right to be critical. Even my resolutely urban surroundings suggest vastness compared to any Tokyo neighborhood. Goodness knows Americans in all kinds of places have had no compunction about pulling up trees to build their dream houses, even when there's enough space to leave a few. A part of me says, Have some tenderness for the houses made to fit different-sized dreams. To which, with chagrin, I admit resistance on the grounds of taste. And to camouflage the chagrin, I think, against everything I know, that in (some) beginning taste was democratically granted by instinct: the instinct to avoid exposure, to seek shelter for the vulnerable shelter erected by merely human hands. To build to the edges of one's lot becomes, accordingly, a willful violation of natural decency.

All this has nothing to do with my grandmother. For her, in a way most of us forget after birth, being is breathing—after two strokes, now more than ever. The new houses with their glittering white, impervious construction material must have seemed suffocating to her. Give her air, light, and earth. The house she built with her hidden savings twenty-some years after the war has deep eaves to shield the rooms from summer sun and monsoon and typhoon rains. Apart from closets, every bit of wall is carved out with windows and sliding glass doors. Even the storage room has large windows. And yet the effect is not one of brittle brightness. On the sunniest days the light shines in on earthen walls, wood, and woven mats.

It wouldn't do to romanticize old Japanese houses, of which this is an updated version. The kitchens typically faced north and guaranteed months of frigid labor for women. In fact, they guaranteed constant labor of all kinds for women, at the same time that they supported a wealth of artisanal labor. The latter is too costly now. The sum my grandmother had squirreled away from my grandfather could not have built their house a scant five years later, given the economic shifts following the successive oil crises. The built-in cost for replacements, such as the rush mats, became prohibitive for her. More and more Japanese will never experience the periodic sensuous explosion of bare foot meeting firm textured ground, eyes resting on quiet sea-green, and above all nostrils invaded by the scent of freshly woven rush. And they will not live within wood that insulates yet breathes, and eventually rots. Nor should they, not at the cost of further clearcutting of North American or any other forests.

What am I mourning, then? A miscellany uncapturable by a name. But, elaborating what was condensed into a sigh or a few mumbled words from my grandmother, I want to trace a path between the desire to exchange interior space for the open air and character. Character as produced within a historical culture now almost unavailable.

The other day, in that most beautiful light of late afternoon, I rediscovered the velvet texture of old, darkened wood. The bare earth, now also rare in Tokyo, covered at most with traces of moss, the literal ground of many Japanese gardens, offers another kind of soft darkness.

Why are these qualities precious? Urban life is filled with materials, objects, and devices that reflect, echo, throw us back upon selves also rendered impervious: chrome, glass, tile, concrete, parking lots, answering machines, all the green dials that stare into the dark. Wood and earth absorb. The character I'm groping for might be called depth. Or repose. Which leaves room for mutuality.

BICYCLES

I've been borrowing my granduncle's bicycle. My grandmother's youngest brother, on the downhill side of seventy, is busier than ever as the reluctant but conscientious head of the old neighborhood association. The bicycle is especially useful in covering the territory when he needs to tack up posters announcing fire drills, funerals, children's summer outings. His busyness must account for the surprise that awaited me on my first bicycle ride this summer. I didn't know, because I couldn't believe, that my hand was the source of the long screech that crescendoed as I careened into corners. I was embarrassed.

From My Grandmother's Bedside

When I was growing up, most bicycle brakes emitted magnificent squeals. Mine did not, never being used enough to require oiling. I envied the boys who tore through the streets, managing dazzling stops to the accompaniment of a piercing screeeeeech just inches before crashing into a car. Now, cool fifth-grade boys turn and stare as I do the same, only lamely. Why would my uncle, careful with equipment as with people, the essence of reserve, permit his bicycle to call such attention to him?

From the earliest days of memory, my uncle visited every afternoon, five or six days a week. He was the Technician (so referred to on telephone inquiries from customers) of my grandparents' photography business. My great-grandmother died when he was two, so my grandmother, the eldest of the siblings, raised him, and he became part of the family enterprise. Ostensibly, then, he had reason to come over every day. He sat for long hours, especially when business was bad. One cup of tea and a sweet was all he would ever have. He was comfortable in his sister's silence, and I think she was happy to have him sit in her house, sometimes reading the paper, but mostly just sitting. Agewise he is more my mother's generation—they began to need reading glasses about the same time—but she has never used other than deferential language with him. They would occasionally take up sports, usually to deplore the perennial last place of their favorite ball club. And there was always the weather. And politics. One day twenty years ago, the three of them set out together to join a group of citizens at the home of the governor of Tokyo, Minobe Ryōichi, in an effort to persuade him to run for a third term.

Minobe was the crowning glory of the left-liberal swing in urban politics of the late 1960s and 1970s, as the cost of high-growth economics became increasingly evident. He tackled the poisonous air and suffocating garbage. He introduced free public transportation and medical care for the elderly. Conservative politicians scorned him as a man devoted to women and children. Perhaps exhilarated by their success with the governor, my grandmother, granduncle, and mother embarked on other political missions, and occasionally baseball games. It might have been the happiest time in the lives of this odd trio.

Since my grandmother became bedridden, I, too, have sat with my uncle in the late afternoon. I commiserate with him about the emergence of soccer as the sport of preference for young boys, thus imperiling his neighborhood baseball club. Now that he heads the neighborhood association, he is too busy to coach the team, and perforce too busy to sit for hours in his sister's house. So I can't tell whether busyness is indeed the reason he has allowed his handbrakes to squeak, or whether the brakes are signalling subterranean shifts that will some day rise to the surface. I try to be more careful than usual about parking the bicycle in the right direction and covering it with the new grey bicycle cover he has bought for it.

THE HOUSE NEXT DOOR

I ring the bell at the gate of our next-door neighbor. No answer. I peer over the closed metal slats set in the fine stone wall. No stirrings in the once white, now greying concrete house.

From My Grandmother's Bedside

All sliding doors and windows are shuttered or reveal drawn curtains. The bay windows are the only transparency amid the grey fastness. These windows, a popular feature of domestic design for a decade or two, stage a version of family identity different from the name plate next to the principal entry. In enticing contrast to the latter, bay windows are governed by the aesthetic of cuteness, being filled with such girl items as dolls, usually "western"; paper or fabric flower arrangements, again "western"; cleverly crafted animals; and lots and lots of lace and frills.

My grandmother's house and her neighbor's are separated by a cinder-block wall. Our side of the wall is lined by a row of tall camellia bushes—trees, really, bought by my older aunt in Nagasaki. The camellias had replaced a common hedge bush, the Japanese cypress, whether out of necessity or vanity I do not know. When I was growing up, the two lots were separated by a simple bamboo latticework fence with Japanese cypresses growing on both sides. There was so much space between the bamboo poles and the low cypresses, and the wooden gate between the two gardens swung so easily, that my best friend and I hardly noticed we were crossing boundaries as we called out for each other's company. "Calling out" was what children literally did outside each other's doors, in a special rhythm and intonation, in the days when streets were filled with children's play. By the late 1950s, the fires of the "entrance examination hell" stoked the success of cram schools; cars and television combined to drain the streets and make the call obsolete.

Several days before fruitlessly ringing my neighbor's bell, I dreamt I was inside their garden and running alongside their house to our backyard, just as I had done many times with my friend. In the dream I seemed to know that I had not called out and that the wooden gate was gone, so I ran with anxiety and awoke with guilt for having trespassed.

Later that day, I thought to use the stiff glossy camellia leaves to dislodge the snails that had appeared on the street side of my grandmother's white garden wall. The night before, my granduncle had come to warn us of the snails that had come out in the extended monsoon to cling to the wall under the fluorescent street lamps. Theirs was a sickly gleam, to be sure, but why their appearance prompted my granduncle's warning escaped me. Knowing my mother's fear and loathing, however, I went out to see what I could do—just in time, since my grandaunt was already hard at work shaking the soft, tenacious bodies into a little mound of salt, a grave of dissolution. Resigned to snail removal as a new task, I was congratulating myself on my new technique when my friend's mother approached from behind and greeted me with surprise and genuine warmth. I looked so young compared to her daughter, she said. I must not have any cares. Her daughter had married into a family that operated a kindergarten, and she had had to take over the management early on.

I had spoken with this modestly elegant woman perhaps once in the last three decades.

My friend and I had been separated when we were ten and our families feuded. Until then, we had played almost every day since the age of three. It was my grandmother who, one rainy day, went next door and brought her piggyback to play

with me. Thereafter we were inseparable until school inter-
fered. Especially in summer, we had our meals together, at my
house. My first lesson in jealousy came when her relatives visited.

Like so many other families in the late 1950s and 1960s, my
friend's family had built tiny rental units atop their living quarters when they renovated their house. In recent years Japanese
officials have taken to bewailing the low birthrate and wondering out loud about the benefits of higher education for
women, but in the postwar years babies abounded in Japan like
everywhere else. And Japanese economic recovery meant the
emptying of the countryside into the cities, and above all into
Tokyo. Housing was in short supply; good money was to be
made in providing excruciatingly modest six-mat rooms with
shared cooking and toilet facilities. (The occupants of such
rooms expected to go to public baths.)

My friend's family built right up to the edge of their property. From what I absorbed, they evidently built to legal excess
in proportion to their land. To avoid difficulties, they claimed
to have made arrangements with my family. My family claimed
that no such discussions had taken place. But more funda-
mentally, I suspect that we, including my aunt next door who
had married and built a house in the backyard, were upset by
the ungainly structure looming over their homes, inhabited by
people we didn't know. My aunt said some of them tossed
trash out the window that landed on our property. Their windows had no blinders, and the grown-ups in our family felt ex-
posed to unseen eyes. Corrugated white plastic blinders went

up to a stipulated height. Then, to conceal the blinders, my aunt planted a row of plain pasania trees, followed by a row of white birches, unusual because unsuited to Tokyo's climate.

The structure next door was wood, painted white. The paint began to peel in a few years. I missed my friend's company. Without anyone telling us that we couldn't play any more, we understood that the friendship was over. Once we happened to glimpse each other through the latticework and walked un-hesitatingly to the fence. We didn't say anything, but I remem-ber, as if in a dream, that my friend smiled at me as if nothing had happened.

I missed my friend, but I also missed her old house and the strip of land behind it, adjacent to our backyard. It was not planted, and the weeds of summertime only made it more en-ticing. A large window in their back room overlooked this space, and I picture my friend's mother sitting in it, perhaps smoking—something no woman in my family did—and laughingly watching us. I was only in their house once or twice. I'm sure it's a child's smallness that makes me remember it as a capacious old Japanese house, much like ours but tantaliz-ingly different and especially inviting in summer. Their garden, too, even though it didn't compete with my grandmother's, in-trigued me with perennials we didn't have.

Their kitchen faced the narrow path between our houses, and running along it at dusk for no particular reason, I could hear my friend's mother's cooking noises. My friend was the youngest of four children, and that too was wonderfully novel for me, an only child and for many years an only grandchild. I liked the sound of dishes clattering and voices rising in inattentive but amiable exchange. My friend's mother did a lot of frying, as my family observed with, I suppose, tacit disapproval. Frying made a lot of noise, and I liked being touched by their family life through the drama of a sizzling wok.

Sometimes, once in a rare while, as I make my way through the early morning streets, I can hear breakfast clatter and smell grilling fish. It suffuses me with a sense of well being, even though I wouldn't dream of preparing such a breakfast myself, certainly not at home, where we have eaten toast since I can remember. Maybe fragrant breakfasts are still being prepared in many homes today, only discreetly, inaccessibly, far behind the closed garage doors.

My friend's family eventually dismantled the house with the apartment units and built the silent structure I peer into over the gate. It looks in much better shape than the house my grandmother built with her modest savings. Until now, I've never thought to ask myself if I haven't been smug about coming from a family that wouldn't think of building in order to rent. I've cherished my grandmother's modesty of wants and needs. And there is something in me that recoils before the robust appetite that fueled Japanese economic growth.

My grandmother's lived aesthetic is consonant with her retiring nature. In two of her daughters that inheritance became a reluctance or refusal to mingle with the world, which inevitably informed their childrearing. Witness my having dined only once or twice at my friend's house.

The three houses that have successively occupied the lot next door tell one aspect of Tokyo postwar history. The two houses I have lived in could be called another version, but they might also be taken as the expression of a step aside from the path of history.

The day after my failed attempt, I ring the doorbell, or rather press the buzzer again. After my encounter with her mother, my friend came to visit, bearing gifts that included a boxed pair of that most prized of summer gifts, the musk melon, complete with golden seals, certificate, and stamped date indicating optimal consumption date, for my grand-mother. I missed the visit, so I want to ask my friend's mother for her telephone number. Eventually—the consequence of the dignified gait of age—a low voice issues from the box on the stone wall. My friend's mother comes out and once again greets me with courtesy and warmth.

THE POSTWAR GARDEN

Why hadn't I noticed her elegance forty years ago? Because I was a child? Meaning both that an adult might not bother to be elegant with a child and that elegance was an aspect of being beyond a child's perception? I don't entirely believe either. I think rather that most people's elegance might take a leave of absence before the demands of four children to be raised in a war-ravaged land.

In those days, on our side of the bamboo fence, there was neither soft mossy earth punctuated with stepping stones, nor shady trees, nor overflowing flower beds, but simply dirt—dirt that was ready to turn into mud after every rain shower, and all the more so after the snowfalls that were common in those days. One day a truck came and dumped a load of cinders in the yard. The cinders were packed down and there was general rejoicing at the prospect of a mud-free life.

It was still more yard than garden. One side was bounded by the Mountain, an air-raid shelter camouflaged with shrubs and flowering plants. The shrubs were mostly azaleas with a few fragrant daphnes and a too-vigorous rhododendron. The flowers were postwar flowers: hollyhocks, gladiolas, sweet williams, cosmos, snapdragons: flowers that could flourish neither in my grandmother's garden, once she was able to buy sun-hogging cherry and magnolia trees, nor in shops, once tastes shifted to more exotic flora. The shelter itself had begun to fill with water, and my friends and I were strictly forbidden its exploration. My father built a tool shed that backed into its outer wall. On the side by the bamboo fence a hen house sat under the persimmon tree. At its peak it housed five hens, raised from chicks brought by kind friends from the countryside. For a time they contributed eggs to our diet, but the ones who survived ended up as pets and just consumed feed. There was also a dog house built by my father for a black pup named Pal, a strange sound for rolling off Japanese tongues. On the other end of the yard, the main street side, was the well, an antique specimen with a squeaky handle but still used by my grandfather for his morning ablutions and my grandmother for watering her plants.

There was all this and a grape arbor too, but my memory from that period is of barren, cinder-filled ground. And one day, upon that hard ground, my father put up a swing for me. It was a post-and-lintel construction of rough-hewn beams. Erected starkly against the bare branches of the persimmon tree, it could have been an execution platform, but the wooden slab hung by sturdy rope attracted my cousins from across the street as well as my friend next door. They were all advanced swingers, unafraid to sail into the sky upright, while I could barely pump myself a foot or two above the ground. When I got rope burn, my father changed the woven straw to rubber hose, which turned out to be equally sturdy, and much easier on the palms.

He must have been handy, knowledgeable in a way no one else in the family was. Years later, I learned that after Pal contracted distemper, my father unplugged one end of the hose from the kitchen gas burner and thrust it into Pal's mouth.

I did not learn until I was nearly twenty that Pal was buried in the backyard. The grown-ups had forgotten they had told me how well Pal was doing in the hospital. And they had not noticed that I understood not to ask when they stopped volunteering reports.

THE HISTORY CONTAINED IN ANIMALS

I wonder what my grandmother thought when my father brought Pal home. (And why did he claim that whimpering pup in the first place? Was it for me, fated to be an only child? Did he know that? Or was it for him, for the same reason? I don't know enough about him except to speculate in generalities.) After Pal, she never allowed dogs in the house. My aunt next door tried twice, and both times she had to return the creature whence it came. The reason my grandmother gave was the death of Kuro ("black"), the prewar family dog, which was

so sad that she vowed never again. Did she think it pointless
to protest to my six-foot-two-plus American father about the
black Japanese dog with an American name?

Kuro's most famous feature was his embarrassingly insistent
bark whenever the chimney sweep or the charcoal dealer came.
That story was always told without irony. No stories grew
around Pal. Mimi the cat (the family imagination for animal
names taking a grand leap to *La Bohème*) evacuated with the
family to escape the fire bombings. She learned to accompany
my mother and her sisters to the house where they bathed,
wait for them, and stand outside the door as soon as she heard
the heavy lid being placed back on the tub. Back in Tokyo,
Mimi died at a ripe old age from eating a poisoned mouse. She
died under the house next door, not my friend's but the one
on the other side. The grown-ups said that cats customarily
went away to die; they seemed to be intimating it was an aspect of their decency.

Mimi, who certainly knew a thing or two about food
scarcity (what made the family bring a cat back to Tokyo in
1946?), must have been well fed by the time of her demise. The
successor tomcats, the offspring of the frightful-looking but
sweet-natured tortoise-shell my granduncle kept, lived during
the best years, when food was plentiful but not yet exorbitant
as it would be after the oil crises of the 1970s. Every day the
tomcats had fresh fish bought and prepared just for them by
my grandmother. The younger one was occasionally indulged
with ice cream.

My grandmother took care of them all. Goldfish with spots
were isolated in mild salt water until they were ready to rejoin

the tank. The finches, the canary, the rare red-beaked spar-row—brought over by one or the other aunt, from generosity or from their own inability to live up to an initial enthusi-asm—were all kept clean and given their special as well as generic food. The older tom, Kuri ("chestnut"), left when the younger one, who had been weaned too early from the sweet ugly tortoise-shell, tried to nurse off him. After a two-year ab-sence he came home with a wicked wound on his right hind leg. He allowed my grandmother to clean it, then came home every day for thirteen days until the wound was healed. Then he disappeared forever.

My aunt in Nagaski told me quite recently that her mother had also roasted sparrows during the war. We had barbecued sparrows in the country, she said, with a hidden note of ac-cusatory triumph. I had never heard that story, though my mother had told often enough of all the forms of sweet potato consumed, the occasional serving of rice stretched with soybean-skin filler. I try to picture my grandmother roasting the sparrows. She would have been grave but matter-of-fact, just as when she treated Kuri's leg, cleaned the sewer trap, or tasted food of dubious age before serving it to any of us.

LABOR

Over the past week changing my grandmother has taken extra time. For the first time in three-and-a-half years of being bed-ridden she has developed a bedsore, and everyone says it's important to make it heal while it's small. Of course, I want to say. The question is how.

We've experimented with two kinds of moisture-proof bandages. They're both expensive, but the slightly less expensive brand rolls up on itself just as you try to stick it on. So we've settled for the other one, normally about a dollar and a quarter each, but now on sale for slightly under a dollar. The nice young dermatologist left a bottle of an expensive cream, a silver compound as far as I can make out, and I went to her clinic on another rainy day with a sterile jam jar to pick up cotton balls immersed in disinfectant. Cotton balls, it turns out, aren't available in ordinary pharmaceutical or cosmetics shops, though cotton in every other imaginable form is. Along with flowers, my aunt next door brought over a little pile of handmade cotton balls. She said a surgeon taught her how to make them once when she had an infection. Then the Clinic Nurse, who visits once a week, showed us how to do it ourselves: take two or three pieces of cotton, pile them together, fluff them out, then give a firm twist at the end, or else the balls bloat into shapeless masses in the disinfectant. The cotton balls floating in the disinfectant the dermatologist gave me have retained their shape beautifully after five days. I can't—don't want to—believe they are handmade.

We bought three new tweezers for fishing out these balls before finding the right kind, but that is another story. The tweezers are sterilized once a day.

When the sore finally healed, I was inclined to credit the silver compound cream.

SHOPPING

We decide to have cold tea-flavored noodles for lunch. Alas, my mother doesn't have my favorite condiments on hand: *shiso* and *myōga*, for which my dictionary only offers the unappetizing translations of "beefsteak plant" and "Zingibar Mioga." The former is much like basil; the latter is unlike anything I know. These two flavors, plus citron, are what I've come to miss most about Japanese cooking when I'm away.

Never mind, I'll go get some at the co-op, I say to my mother.

Even now, I would guess that only a minority of households do all their grocery shopping in one exhausting swoop over the weekend. When I was very little, in the days when my mother was bedridden with tuberculosis and again later when she didn't want to go out branded with the signs of a failed marriage, my grandmother dashed out most days before both lunch and dinner. She had to go no more than five minutes in three directions—"gutter's edge," "up," or "market"—to find an assortment of fresh fish, vegetables, prepared foods, and dry goods. At "gutter's edge," meaning next to the river-turned-sewer-turned-cherry-tree-lined-walk (another story of the Olympics-hastened modernization of Tokyo), there was a fish store. Going "up," meaning turning left at the gate and walking ever so slightly uphill from the house, got you to a green grocer. "Market" referred to a hodgepodge of stores further "down" from the house, where everything in the way of unfancy food was available along with a pharmacy and a flower shop.

In those shops the only aesthetic was that of fresh food piled with little concern other than for mechanical balance. All these institutions, the stopgap salvation of my grandmother's busy days, have disappeared. But there are plenty of similar shops, as well as supermarkets and twenty-four-hour "convenience" (*kombini*) stores, especially on those streets leading away from the train stations. Several generations of women can be found stopping at five, six, seven, even eight o'clock, buying fresh or, more likely at the later hours, tasty enough prepared foods. Tokyo is still Old Worldly—more than ever, in some respects—because of a nostalgia fed by wealth for that which has never been experienced.

FUEL DRAMA

You turn left at the public bath to get to the "market." I noticed for the first time last night, no doubt many years after the fact, that the space next to the public bath had turned into a parking lot. What used to be there? I couldn't dredge up the image. My mother says it was a gas station.

But the gas station, owned by the public bath, had started a fire. (I have always found the tall chimneys of public baths eerie, not so different from those of crematoria rising here and there against the city skyline. These are for normal use, but after Auschwitz, even the coincidence of form . . .) So the bath had shut down the gas station and produced that most innocuous of real-estate money makers, guilty merely of contributing to air toxicity, a parking lot.

It wasn't a good place for a gas station anyway. It was too quiet. In Japanese gas stations, the tanks are set in the ceiling and the hoses dangle down. Maybe there are self-service pumps, but I haven't seen any. Self-service would dampen the ethos. A good deal of whooping accompanies the arrival and departure of cars. To leave with a full tank is a bit like stepping out of a decent hotel in, say, New York to get into a taxi. One of the young men uniformed in California colors steps into the street, whistles and gesticulates, and creates a miraculous opening in the stream of traffic to allow the customer's car a grand entry.

That would have been absurd on the street corner leading to the "market."

CONVERSATION

She began talking last night while we were changing her. I said it was getting late, almost time to turn on the news show hosted by Kume Hiroshi, the erstwhile "idol of intellectual middle-aged women," as a friend once described him. "I know who that is," piped up my grandmother. Then she said she was not sleepy.

My mother jumped to the head of the bed and embraced her tenderly. I had thought she was remarkably impervious to my grandmother's loss of speech following the second stroke. I was unkindly and self-protectively inclined to attribute her continued capacity to give unstinting care to a certain insensitivity.

That morning my grandmother had looked at me as if for the first time.

—Where have you been?

—Upstairs.

No answer.

—Didn't you know I was here? I came from Chicago to be with you.

—Did you swim over?

—No, I didn't swim. I took an airplane.

—Oh . . . It's hot downstairs, isn't it?

—No. You know, it's always cooler downstairs. Besides, it's raining today.

—Oh. Did you get wet?

—No, I didn't get wet.

Then, when the Home Helper arrived, she was able to say good morning and pronounce her name. As if she had awakened for the first time in three months.

After the weekly visiting bath had come and gone, she was tired. She would nod in response to questions but would no longer speak.

My grandmother's legs are apt to tremble whenever we are doing something with her. We have been taught to hold them firmly. It's as if she were terror-stricken, but that is our logic. I say, objectively, It's just a neurologic response. The Home Helper says, It's Obaachama's way of expressing herself. My mother said to her this afternoon, It's all right, you don't need to shake. To which my grandmother said, It's better for me to shake.

In the golden twelve hours since last night, she has said a number of things that I couldn't understand. I thought, We'll have to work harder to understand her new speech.

So much of her care is like the care of an infant, of course.

But she has not spoken all afternoon. I begin to wonder if we'll need to learn to decipher her sounds after all. Whether we'll have the opportunity.

Speech is often taken to be a, or the, defining characteristic of human beings.

I had not known how transformed is the face of the un-speaking adult.

DEATH AND EMBARRASSMENT

I am never, ever embarrassed by her. And I am not embarrassed at her being seen by anyone. But I would be pained if a friend, acquaintance, or stranger were to be embarrassed by her.

Like most people, I used to avert my eyes, figuratively if not physically, when I found myself in the presence of persons with deformities. My grandmother has removed many, though not all, of my fears about deformity and incapacitation.

My mother puts on a tape of my daughter playing Mozart's Andante in C for Flute. It's a young girl's playing, faltering and yet charming. My grandmother listens avidly, as if she were posing for a statue of Woman Listening to Music. When it is over, I ask if she remembers her great-granddaughter. She nods, yes. Does she like listening to this tape?

—I love it.

From My Grandmother's Bedside

With her eyes, she searches the room for the girl who shares her name.

And this act evokes for me another, that of my dog when the name of his dog-friend is uttered. Is this a cruel turn of mind? I examine it gingerly and come out safe. It doesn't matter if, in effect, there's a resemblance between the discontinuities of my grandmother's mind and the continuities of my dog's. My care is inspired by the memory of the person who cared for and loved me. And it is also inspired by the charm of the person who emerged transformed by stroke. The latter is sheer luck. Or is it?

My grandmother's life is sustained by a nasal feeding tube. Three times a day, she receives a nutritious liquid diet that comes in two flavors, vanilla and chocolate. She will never taste the vanilla flavor that my mother unhesitatingly selects for her.

For over a year after her first stroke, my grandmother's right wrist was tied to the bed railing. This was because she had managed to pull her feeding tube out a number of times, throwing my mother into a panic. My mother was gentle, first wrapping the wrist in a gauze handkerchief, then looping a cloth string in a special way the nurses taught her so as not to bind, and then securing the other end to the side-railing. Sometimes this was done with apologies, but it was always done.

For a long time I misread the name of the liquid diet as "Endure" rather than "Ensure."

Friends have asked me, Would your grandmother have wanted this? *Would have wanted*: our verb forms reach for the boundaries of the knowable and draw them in. But I can no longer answer, Of course not, the way I would have four years ago. I do know it would be hasty to say, She tries to remove the tube because she doesn't want to go on living.

"Death with dignity" has become a catchphrase in Japan over the past few years. This is, after all, the longest-lived society in the world, with a shrinking population of the young—the long decrescendo from the baby boom. The state, meanwhile, is busily privatizing. Given the alarming demographic trends, recent governments proclaim their intent to ensure that burdens on citizens will not become intolerable over the next few decades. Now, while the citizen as taxpayer may be relieved by the state's fiscal virtue, the same citizen as person, more often than not an aging woman like my mother, is crushed by the physical and psychological burden of caring for still older parents and in-laws.

Everyone I know who has cared for an elderly parent or watched friends do so has said she does not want to be a burden for her children. I also say the same. I say, I cannot do for my mother what she is doing for hers, and I wouldn't expect it of my daughter.

Do we mean it? Isn't it at least as hard to imagine our own senility as it is our death?

DEATH AND SHAME

The state is doing its duty to citizens by reducing their tax burdens for the care of the elderly. By divesting itself of these and other responsibilities for social welfare, it is behaving responsibly. It averts future shame for fiscal laxity.

Forty-some French citizens residing in Japan have signed a petition addressed to Jacques Chirac urging him to cancel plans for the resumption of nuclear testing. At the same time, they are appealing to Japanese citizens to protest more actively.

With the Upper House elections coming up (on July 23), some prominent politicians have called for, or rather suggested the usefulness of, a boycott of French goods.

Now there's a challenge. Japan is a leading importer of French luxury goods. The sentimental education of a human being as consumer favors the transcendence of political passions. That is, passions become biases, to be overcome, for better and for worse, like other biases. Of course, nuclear tests and Vuitton bags have nothing to do with each other.

Over the postwar half-century, it has become increasingly difficult for most Japanese to continue to feel the horror of nuclear bombs. The cold war didn't help: the principal antinuclear organizations had to maintain their credibility while justifying testing by the U.S. and its allies in the free world but not by the Soviet Union, or vice versa, depending on their alignments. China and France added complicating chapters to that story. Successive governments in Japan, packaged by the U.S. as the pillar of freedom in the Far East, worked to desensitize Japanese to their nuclear "allergy," both as part of the long-term project of becoming a "normal" nation with military capability and the more immediate project of promoting reliance on nuclear energy. And above all, postwar Japanese have been busy, busy, busy. Busy rebuilding and building factories, houses, bridges, amusement parks, high-speed trains; busy going to school and cram school; busy playing computer games to relax before more study; busy drinking after hours as part of the work day; busy commuting; busy crawling out of the "loan hell" into which the lucky ones tumble for the privilege of having a home of one's own to commute from; busy fighting crowds during holiday travel. Busy learning the pleasures of the economic miracle, or rather learning to register as pleasures the experiences it has afforded. All the while blunting the intuition that there might be no relaxing after a miracle.

Is the capacity to shed the past a trait favored by evolution? Can we grow, and regrow, membranes that respond to pain removed in time and space, membranes that will not adapt to a televisual sensory overload?

French Polynesia, which will be wounded by the testing (pace Chirac), occupies a part of the Pacific far from the Japanese archipelago. The latter contains Hiroshima and Nagasaki, names at least that are not forgotten, as well as multiple reactors, whose names bob to the surface of the sea of information at the time of accidents, only to disappear within a day or two.

The Only Country in the World has responsibilities to the world.

Instead: a prudent government, weary citizens-turned-consumers, and a silent archipelago.

As her days of speechlessness accumulate, my grandmother's lips turn into thin lines.

And seal me into numbness.

From My Grandmother's Bedside

KINDS OF ENDING

The sound of the monsoon rain is as relentless as white noise. It seeps into the grain of the tatami floor, the wooden beams, the earthen walls. On the doors of the bedding closet next to my grandmother's room, a stain creeps up the fabric covering. The stain has nothing to do with the rain, and it is in fact unlikely to be creeping, up or down. But during the monsoon limbs turn spongy and the mind molds over. Rain, rain, world without end.

The monsoon could infect even a child with weariness sufficient unto death. I can still conjure up the way the glass panels of the verandah doors, my grandmother's apron, the ghostly forest of laundry hanging from the ceiling, used to take on the same indifferent chill.

Terminal lassitude. Is that what keeps my grandmother moaning now, day and night?

On a sunlit afternoon, the stain would echo the worn straw color of the tatami, and death would be a clean, dry withering.

GARBAGE

I heard water being drawn from the garden well, then splashed on the ground from a pail. I looked at my watch. 4:15. In mild disgust I willed myself back to sleep.

At 7:30 I said to my mother, accusingly: What were you doing up at four this morning?

—I was putting out the garbage. Then I poured water down the street because there was a disgusting puddle at the corner.

Her tone is more righteous than defensive. She has always complained about the bad drainage around our house. Water doesn't gather around anyone else's house. Something dubious about the public works project that worked on the drainage here.

I won't be diverted so easily.

—But why did you have to do it at four?

—It wasn't four. It was five.

—No it wasn't. I looked at my watch.

—I looked at my watch. I wear my watch all night long.

—So do I. Your eyes are bad. You read five for four.

—Oh. So I cheated myself an hour.

No battle this time. I know that my mother's insistence on being the first on the block to put out the garbage led to an epic fight with her sister, possibly a permanent breach. Garbage ends sororal relationship.

After dinner, I do the dishes while my mother waits for my grandmother's liquid diet to finish dripping from the bag suspended from an old coathanger hook (all the while anxiously adjusting the speed), tells her that she's going to brush her teeth for the last time that day, wipes her face, then takes a shower herself. After that, we usually have dessert.

My mother has picked up an exhausting miscellany of information. Example: they say you're supposed to stop eating three hours before you go to sleep. But I eat until the minute I fall asleep.

She does, beginning with a chocolate-covered cherry. Too sweet, she says, then picks up a soy-sauce flavored rice cracker. Then a slice of cake comes out of the freezer. Then peanuts.

The principle of alternating sweet and salt has no internal logic of cessation. Only sleep will do it.

She was always small. Now, halfway into her fourth year of caring for her mother, she weighs barely ninety pounds.

The other day, she brought out from the refrigerator a small pile of beautifully packaged desserts of kiwi, cherry, strawberry, pineapple, orange, or mango in gelatin or cream and said, Let's have these tonight. After we had each consumed two (four different kinds), she said with deep satisfaction as she swept up the empty containers, Now these are in time for the Noncombustible Trash Pickup tomorrow.

REASON AND DEMENTIA

A friend is struggling with the onset of dementia in her mother, long suffering from Parkinson's disease. She and her siblings decided to hospitalize her because she had begun to roam, as they say. (The Japanese word *haikai suru* could also be translated as *to wander*. But "wandering" in English has a psychological sense that is too inviting in this context, while lacking the irony of a word that preeminently conjures up space, at least to the American mind trained by "Home on the Range." The demented adult implodes space somewhat as a toddler does. Which is to say that when we are deemed competent, most of our movements are harmless.) My friend's quandary was that the standard sort of facility available in her region was a psychiatric ward, where, as my friend put it, she would be caged. So they found a less restrictive setting, which meant that the sisters had to take turns spending the day watching their mother. For one or another reason, as usually happens, the hoped-for rotation of sisters failed to materialize, and my friend has ended up making the arduous drive every day. The mother has to be coaxed by her daughter to take a single step on her own. Isn't it strange, says the nurse. The problem is, at night she gets out of bed on her own and starts roaming.

Many years ago, I remember the grown-ups speaking with sympathy of a daughter-in-law in a relative's family. The mother-in-law had not only taken to roaming but was telling neighbors that she wouldn't dream of taking medicine from her son, a prominent nephrologist, because it was sure to be poisoned.

This morning an acquaintance in Okinawa tells me about her uncle who, as a boy, survived the "iron typhoon" of the Battle of Okinawa and eventually found a job in the U.S. Occupation bureaucracy. By 1972, when the islands reverted to Japanese administration, he was on the verge of retirement. He was then confronted with a new set of supervisors: young men fresh out of Tokyo University, beginning their careers in the elite national bureaucracy with service in the hinterland of Okinawa. Caught between them and the still fiery unions, the would-be retiree became, in the words of his physician niece, neurotic. Every morning, before setting out for work, he wailed to his wife, Mother, Mother, what am I supposed to do? He is a little senile now, says his niece. He goes out on his bicycle, weaving this way and that in the middle of the high-way, never minding the ever-lengthening trail of cars honking behind him.

My grandmother has been tested twice to determine her de-gree of disability. The first test was short and simple. She was asked to name the day of the week, her age, the current prime minister, and the date of the end of the Pacific War, among other things. Evaluation: strong possibility of a degree of dementia. What compensation has she found?

EDUCATION

The woman with the happily cycling uncle is contemplating becoming an ordinary mother, by which she means going through the examination war with her son as he prepares for university. (He has not yet begun high school.) I am resolved to be hated by him for the rest of my life, she says. We will both shed blood, but if he ends up shedding less than I, it will have been worth it.

How many women can describe as clearly what it means to become an "examination mama," I ask.

Oh, many, she says.

FUNERAL GEAR I: FORD MOTOR CO.

Coming home from outings, it is customary in my family to ask the cab driver to take a left at the Ford sign. Through all the episodes of trade war threat, the light has never gone out of the big blue sign with the white Detroit script glowing in my part of the Tokyo night sky.

The other day, I walked by the circular, glassed-in showroom. There were only two cars. One of them was a hearse.

The body of a Japanese hearse is a plain black limousine. The top looks like a miniature shrine in gold. Strange, when you think of it, since Shinto abhors pollution and the division

· 53 ·

of cultural labor for the most part assigns the dead to the custody of Buddhist priests and temples.

The golden part of this particular hearse was covered with a neat-fitting canvas top. Was it in for repairs? Surely it wasn't for sale? Is Ford creative enough to make limousines usable as hearses in Japan? More likely, and more pertinent: once upon a time, Japanese saw that American cars offered the necessary space and signified the requisite luxury for conversion into hearses.

FUNERAL GEAR II: GIRLS

In the news: A high-school teacher in Fukuoka slapped a girl several times in the face, causing her to fall against a concrete pillar. She died the same day of brain injuries, just before the start of summer vacation. The teacher slapped her because she had allegedly refused when told that, because she did not need to take the make-up test about to be administered, she should leave the room. But some say the teacher actually became enraged when he saw that she had rolled her waistband over, in effect shortening her skirt.

The girl's father sobbed to the television interviewer that he had not known what kind of school he had been sending his daughter to. The school, an all-girls' school, was known for sports and discipline (meaning rules for everything, including hair-ribbon width). During subsequent investigations, nearly half the teachers confessed to engaging in corporal punishment, though it is unambiguously forbidden by the Fundamental Law of Education, an outstanding achievement of the democratizing postwar years. The principal qualified, however, that it was difficult to determine what constituted corporal punishment. Some of the girls said the principal patted them on the butt when greeting them and slapped them if they had their waistbands rolled over. He agreed that such things might have happened from time to time.

The pious inquiry of the media ranges from What do the teachers think they're teaching through violence? and Did the teacher slap for the sake of the pupil or out of frustration? to Didn't the father have a family vacation planned? An American commentator adds to the grotesquerie by trotting out the adage about not hitting in anger and intoning the importance of securing third-party approval before engaging in corporal punishment.

Most commentators refer to the perennial problem, or rather the perennialization of the problem, of *ijime*, student-on-student harassment that at times results in suicide. A few raise another topic endemic to discussions of education, namely the problem of the *naishinsho*, or confidential school recommendation sent from one school to another as the child grows. It is commonly said that the school report holds parents hostage to the school: if you complain about your child's treatment, the teacher will write an unfavorable report, and you will only have hurt your child. But what are the implications of such power for the teacher? Especially in a system where every reform, such as the gradual elimination of Saturday classes, seems only to intensify competition. Pity the drivers of a perpetual race.

As the girl's hearse drove off, her classmates in middy uniforms crumpled upon each other and wailed. Mass hysteria, said a friend, a passionately dedicated junior high school teacher. Her own analysis begins with the difficulty adolescent girls pose for teachers, especially male teachers, with their abhorrence of male "dirtiness"—something that in America today would be captured by the term *sexuality.*

The hearse is extra fancy.

The girls' faces are blurred (through "mosaic imaging") and their voices altered to protect their identity in all interviews. Anonymous Aum sect believers—that is, the rank and file who remain in the sect in spite of multiple arrests after the subway Sarin poisoning episodes and numerous disclosures of science-fiction-like practices of torture and killing such as the use of gigantic microwave ovens in the name of sect discipline—are also protected, regardless of age, through mosaic imaging and voice alteration. More and more, people who are interviewed in connection with incidents in the news are presented mosaically. Has the protection of the individual become a matter of fragmentation into anonymity?

FUNERAL GEAR III: PORTOLETS AND POETRY

The neighborhood temple is rebuilding its funeral hall. Maybe it will be able to host multiple parties at once. Will it remember to leave enough room for parking?

Since people don't postpone their deaths for the renovation of funeral halls, the temple has put up a temporary hut with portolets just outside. The door on the men's side only goes up to waist height.

This Sunday morning, preparations were afoot for a large funeral. My mother, the Home Helper, and I had been grumbling about it because my granduncle of the squeaky bicycle had been designated head of the funeral committee: the greeter and chief eulogizer. Why did he have to take it on? He was so busy, so tired. He had no close ties to the family as far as we knew.

The deceased was in her nineties. She had been a midwife. The claim on my granduncle, it turned out, was that she had delivered his first child. That was on March 10, 1945, the day everyone of a certain age remembers as the day of the fire-bombing of Tokyo. (There were of course many other fire-bombings, but this was the one that turned Tokyo into a flaming sea.)

In her later, leisurely years, the midwife had composed haiku and even published them in a volume. My uncle was given a copy, presumably to help with preparing his remarks. Con-scientiously, he found a poem about grandchildren to read at the ceremony.

After it was safely over, my uncle felt that his selection had been warmly appreciated.

My uncle will always be exhausted. And appreciated.

GHOSTS

With this building, the temple grounds have sacrificed much of their mystery. The temple kindergarten hosts a ghost hunt in late August for the oldest class of children. The fluorescent lamps are turned off, and a few lanterns are strung amongst the ancient trees. (This little section of the neighborhood es-caped bombing.) The teachers paint their faces white and hide in the spacious grounds. Ghost stories were a cooling device before air conditioning. My own daughter claimed not to have been frightened at all, but for several weeks afterward she refused to set foot on the grounds at the first signs of dusk.

In late August and September, my mother and her sisters used to make a paste of grated cucumber and peroxide for their faces. They cut gauze masks to drape over the glistening plaster and terrified me as they went about their tasks. An instant later, I would be repulsed by the smell in their wake. How could the innocuous cucumber have acquired such odor in my memory? The sisters said they were trying to restore their complexions for the fall.

My mother says I'm misremembering. Only the middle sister did that, making up fresh plaster for her face every day to prepare for her wedding two months later.

TEMPLES AND SOCIAL REALISM

I stand breathless before the beautifully developed photographs of the temples of Kyoto and Nara—poster-size photos of eighth-, ninth-, tenth-, and eleventh-century structures and sculptures. The warmth of the wood, whether in pillars or overhanging roof beams, makes me shiver, taking me back to when I was sixteen and first visiting those temples myself.

As for Buddhist sculptures, I have often wanted but failed to be moved by them in museums. But that's probably the case with other religious art (oxymoron of modernity!) as well. It's the contact of toe with centuries-old wooden floor, cool in summer and piercing in fall and winter, the soft dimness of interior, and the stillness of garden, gravel, and earthen wall that seize and quiet us. Or the mute trace of long use by fellow humans on the worn faces of anonymous wayside buddhas.

But in these photographs by Domon Ken (1909–90), I am startled by the dazzle he found in the swirling robe patterns of the slender eighth-century Kannon ("goddess of mercy," a simplified rendition given this bodhisattva's shifting gender). I've seen this statue several times and known what to admire about it, but it was always dark, graceful, and aloof. I know that in getting these shots Domon had all kinds of contraptions and assistants as well as the privilege of being a renowned photographer, but I am still grateful for the brilliance he found in the wood. Take a bodhisattva figure with a thousand hands. These were always curiosities to me, the idea of the work of a thousand hands momentarily arresting, but no more. Domon's camera thrusts the forest of hands at the viewer, the sharp angle producing a dizzying confrontation. Then there's the shot of the hundred Kannon with eleven heads and a thousand hands. Again, where I had been politely wearied, I am now—terrified.

In other words, I'm being taught to see anew. This is one thing art is supposed to do, of course. It isn't what I thought I was seeking in the exhibit, however.

Domon's work is being exhibited and published in a multi-volume edition in conjunction with the fiftieth anniversary of the end of the war. It is a vast oeuvre, extending from the 1930s through the 1970s. I want to say it suggests an omnivorous but focused appetite. He was an ardent exponent of the unposed snapshot ("absolutely unstaged realism," he called it) in which the photographer seized the essence of the subject. Domon also took memorable portraits and landscapes—to which he insisted the principle of unstaged realism applied as well—but I am most drawn to his documentary photography. One shot in his Hiroshima series teaches the expressivity of the human back: the back of a father huddled against a windowsill while a priest, whose dark, massive back fills half the foreground, prays over the body of his son, dead at fourteen after in utero exposure to radiation. The focal point might have been the child's face, but it is covered with a white cloth according to custom. In his Chikuhō coal mine series, the documentarist's eye alights upon a girl intent on reading, or rather pretending to read, a comic book while more fortunate classmates eat their lunches. The national policy shift from coal to oil in the mid-1950s devastated mining communities in southern Japan. Domon had his collection of children and their families living in the shadow of slagheaps printed in a rough, hundred-yen edition to benefit the community.

After he suffered a stroke Domon gave up his 35mm camera and opted for a large 4x5 camera with tripod. This is when he resumed his pilgrimage to old temples, which he had begun in the 1940s and broken off in the later war years. I went to the exhibit of the temple photos because I wanted to know why a man who—from what I could tell from my recent but enthusiastic acquaintance—expended his soul on the great upheavals of the postwar years was so drawn to the world of "classical" Buddhist art. I could not imagine that the familiar narrative of youthful, this-worldly activity ceding naturally (through illness and age) to a quest for religious truth would be pertinent in his case. What I found was a different but hardly uncommon narrative, one much, much harder for me to come to terms with.

The pamphlet from the Ken Domon Museum of Photography in Sakata City in northern Yamagata Prefecture—apparently the only museum in the world dedicated to the work of a single photographer—announces that Domon's art demonstrates an exhaustive command of Japanese beauty, Japanese spirit. I thought to myself, this is just the predictable rhetoric of the hometown museum proud of the local boy who made good. Other parts of the same pamphlet encouraged me in this view. Domon is quoted describing a transformative moment: he had thought, like everyone else, that Buddhist architecture and sculpture, like mountains and trees, were among the more static of photographic objects. But one twilight, after he had packed up for the day, he turned back to bid farewell to the magnificent Phoenix Hall of the Byōdoin Temple, when he saw it racing away at dizzying speed against a backdrop of clouds. "Camera!" he shouted. He managed one shot before the hall disappeared in the dark.

This, I thought, was not a man concerned with Japaneseness.

Domon was a writer of considerable power, and many of the didactic signs in the exhibit quote him directly. Unexpectedly, one seems addressed to me:

> It is my view as a photojournalist that today whether one grapples with immediate social reality or with the classical culture and tradition of Nara or Kyoto makes no difference, as long as one pursues the anger, the sorrow, the joy of the Japanese people—in more general terms, that which touches

upon the fate of the people. If there is a difference, it is on the order, so to speak, of the difference between Western medicine, directed at the symptom, and Chinese medicine, with its slow, sustained approach; but I don't think there is a fundamental difference in critical orientation.

But Japan today has too many problems. A doctor would say there are too many emergency patients. Of course, there's Vietnam; then there's Okinawa [then occupied by the U.S.], the antinuclear movement, pollution, inflation. We need anti-dotes that will work right away; the slow-acting cures might be just too slow. Once the patient dies, there's no medicine to be prescribed. As a photojournalist and witness, I, too, want to grapple with the problems of the day, pronounce indict-ments, and speak out to light a fire. I want to participate with my camera in the struggle of the people.

In any case, what's in question is the guts of the people. Whatever they think, whatever they do, everything becomes meaningless if the Japanese people cease to be Japanese. . . . During my difficult journeys of "pilgrimage to ancient tem-ples," I've been driven to ask myself why I persist with some-thing so laborious. In the end, I arrive at the conclusion that, as a Japanese, I am doing this so that I myself can discover Japan, know Japan, and then report on what I've discovered and learned about Japan to everybody.

The word Domon used for "everybody" [*minna*] here is inti-mate, meaning other Japanese. These passages come from an article written in 1968 titled, precisely, "On Covering Demonstrations and Pilgrimages to Ancient Temples." Why am I so disheartened? There is nothing especially reprehensi-ble in these sentiments. Far from it. I had just hoped for some-thing else, a mode of thinking, a logic of motivation, that wouldn't turn into a circle defined by Japaneseness.

Before embarking on his photography career, Domon had taken part in an agrarian movement, been arrested and tortured several times, and, like the overwhelming majority of leftists and other radicals of the early 1930s, recanted. And again like many others, he became impassioned over questions of social justice in the postwar years. He pursued them not as abstractions but as something embodied in every one of his subjects. Of course, the phenomenon of left nationalism is hardly novel. Anti-Americanism as a mobilizing element of postwar Japanese pacifist movements involving labor, teachers, and students lent a tacitly nationalist coloring to many forms of activism into the early 1970s. Call Domon a critical patriot, a champion of the people. And an artist. Isn't that enough? As with any other artist, his work can't be contained by his own programmatic statements. Like all human beings, he's part of a larger history. As an energetic, enormously talented photographer, he delivers that history with extraordinary vividness.

Still, given the history in question, it's hard not to shrink before Domon's choice of word for people, *minzoku. Minzoku* isn't just people, it's *the* people. Wherever an assortment of human beings are drawn together as *the people,* a transformation takes place. Powerfully good things can be brought forth by it, such as the overthrow of colonial regimes. With a people, energy is amassed that's more than the aggregate of individual energy, different from that of a crowd. (Though a crowd can also become a people.)

Whether a people are convoked as chosen ones on the grounds of birth or of social position should make a difference in how joinable they will be. Yet, the production of a people logically seems to entail the production of a nonpeople. This is understandable during the actuality of oppression, but all too often it proves difficult to shed exclusivity. Even secular identities can transmogrify into natural or divine endowments and, given the right historical conjuncture, do harm to others. The Japanese People, *Nihon minzoku*, were convoked in a world organized by imperialism. Beginning with victory over China (1895) and Russia (1905), the annexation of Korea (1910), and the Manchurian Incident (1937), the Japanese People, whose highest expression was the Emperor, were mobilized to seize and occupy expanses of land on the continent and on islands off Southeast Asia. At least in rhetoric, and for some Japanese in belief, the inhabitants of the occupied lands were called to service as children of the same Emperor. If this made the other Asians into siblings, the Japanese People still came first. They alone were fit to lead Asian children out from under the yoke of Western imperialism. The population that became the Japanese People in this discursively complex but in practice plainly discriminatory way were brutalized, and both enabled and compelled to inflict immeasurable suffering on their neighbors and themselves.

I know this is a partial description of modernity and its consequences for Japan, but it can't be edited out when reading in 1995 Domon Ken's recourse to *minzoku* in 1968. That's why it's disheartening to see Domon's participation in the popular obsession with the uniqueness of Japanese culture.

So there's a politico-historical dimension to my disappointment before the exhibition sign. But viscerally and puerilely, the moment I read his words on the wall next to the spectacular black-and-white photographs of Murōji Temple, I feel left out: these works had never imagined me amongst its viewers! (Knowing that Domon won distinguished prizes abroad, that he took pleasure in having his prints published abroad, doesn't change this.)

But there's something else still, issuing from intersection of the historical and the absurdly personal. I realize I had wanted Domon to model for me a way of loving so-called classical Japanese art without participating in a reactionary or naive cultural exceptionalism. The modernist eye directed at beams, pillars, and brackets, the gleam captured in statues, was appealing, especially because, juxtaposed with his passion for social documentary, I had thought or hoped that it wasn't principally an instrument of apolitical aestheticism.

I had fantasied that Domon would show me a way past my guilty and ill-examined abstinence from the artifacts and, yes, aura of premodern Japanese culture because of their deployment by modern Japan.

COMPLICATIONS

Domon's career began with his employment by the Nihon Kōbō studio. He photographed fishing villages, farms, factories, athletic events, and Tokyo entertainment quarters for *Nippon*, the company's quarterly magazine designed to introduce Japanese culture overseas. There are breathtaking shots of a fisherman framed between sharply arced sails; a line of boys in loincloths jumping off a boat, captured in the instant before slapping the water; sailors in training with oars raised against a sun-sparkling sea. Seeing the striking display of form in these pictures, I'm taken back to the temple shots. He's wrong, I want to say. His art isn't for and about the Japanese People. His subjects happen to be Japanese people.

But of course, he could say his camera lens had turned them into the Japanese People. Moreover, the cult of form is itself part of the cult of Japaneseness. Step back for a minute and argue that Domon's art instantiates a general, modernist formalism. It's no escape. These two arguments can be insidiously linked to reproduce a prewar philosophical claim of Japan and Japanese values as universal, incorporating yet transcending western modernity. But there's a more immediate issue. Domon's photographs of inductees into the Imperial Army, of sailors of the Imperial Navy, of teenagers in kimonos (members of the Girls' Unit of the Youth Flight Corps, lined up for glider training) were disseminated in *Nippon* in the late 1930s as the Japanese offensive on the continent escalated. Printing them with little or no explanatory text minimized the dissonance with the magazine's cultural mission. In this context Domon's work becomes a textbook illustration of how formalism, by obscuring content and repressing historical context to emphasize the beauty of abstract lines, shapes, and contrasts of light and dark, can have a specific political and historical function.

Not that formalism ever completely banishes content. There is plenty of thematic tension in Domon's photos from this period, which in turn feeds the formal fascination. For example, Domon obsessively photographed nurses in training at the school of the Japan Red Cross Society. Besides shots of nurses helping patients to walk, nurses demonstrating bandaging, and nurses paired up for stretcher duty, there are nurses practicing traditional Japanese archery and nurses marching four abreast with halberds. They are dressed in white, full-skirted uniforms with tall, billowing caps only slightly less extravagant than chef's hats. The camera guides the eye to the finger poised at the tip of an arrow, a finger otherwise, presumably, adept at bandaging. Nurses leaving for the front upon graduation dressed in dark coats, hats, stockings, and shoes sip sake before a Shinto altar on the rooftop of the Red Cross headquarters to pray for long-lasting military fortune. Their juniors stand behind, in whites, to send them off. It's possible to think of these photos of healing angels/women warriors as a novel twist on the theme of "Japanese Spirit, Western Learning," itself a variation on "Japanese Spirit, Chinese Learning": formulations whereby Japanese have sought to contain the cost to self-esteem of that most human activity, learning from one's neighbors, so often denigrated as "borrowing" with its implicit charge of unoriginality. But Domon's nurse series is eerie for its brilliant revelation of Domon's fascination, and eerie for its seduction of the viewer. What's so unsettling here? I think it's that Domon's talent makes us complicit in experiencing as beautiful the harnessing of decent human purpose to macabre ends.

The military, sports, factories—like modern artists elsewhere, Domon was drawn to human figures in alignment. Even an ostensibly traditional scene of farm women harvesting rice shows them as a line of dark, bent forms, not initially discernible as human. The formalist Domon was a Japanese poet of the mechanization of human beings.

What about the temples, then? Of course, the question is more complicated than when I posed it out of personal rebuff. It wouldn't be satisfying, politically, aesthetically, or emotionally, to conclude either that the social realist documents, the formalist documents, and the temples are three separate aspects of a prolific artist's oeuvre, or that they are unified by a formalist vision or by a celebratory ethnography. There's an economy of the national and the universal within both the social realist and the formalist works. It isn't possible to simply reject or embrace either pole.

Was my hurt nonsensical? I have to remember that it was Domon's statement about his photographs of Buddhist art that precipitated my little crisis. Our modern understanding of art, inextricable from the history of the individual and of museum ownership, creates the expectation and desire to be in private dialogue with works of art. Hence, the strangeness of the museum space, especially of the art museum: a strangeness possibly capturable by a Buñuel, wherein individuals, often alone, but also in twos and threes, allow themselves to be publicly seen in silent communion with objects. I had grafted this modern relationship—tacitly held as an inalienable right, or really a contract—onto the artifacts of premodern religious institutions. Domon's claim about the Japaneseness of his art and its audience interrupted that presumption, made it visible. But his presumption of a continuity called "Japan" from the eighth century to the postwar is also modern, made possible, or necessary, by the history of nation-states.

I can't unravel the contradictions in Domon's art. It seems invaluable in trying to understand three or four transformational decades of Japanese history. A new acquaintance, also drawn to his art, tells me how rotten Domon was personally, never thinking twice of sending assistants up towers and roofs without a lifeline to hold lights, or to remove centuries' worth of dust—whatever was necessary to produce the perfect un-staged realist shot. And there's a particular horror for me in reading that after his third stroke he lived for eleven years without regaining consciousness.

I find myself coming back to one shot over and over in the summer of the fiftieth anniversary. It is a scene from a send-off party for the master of a confectionary shop and one of his clerks, the first conscripts from the Ginza to be sent to the Chinese front. A long, narrow table is lined with beer bottles and men smiling, holding rising sun flags, preparing to toast the master in the foreground. The men are in suits (the master's associates?) or kimonos (the clerk's?). There are several boys in black school uniforms. Their smiles are more tentative, as if they are learning how to feel from watching their elders. The three girls are dressed up, but their faces are turned away from the camera. Standing in the back, between a man in a three-piece suit with a broad smile and raised glass and a crouching woman with a smile, is an old woman, her right hand holding a flag, her left hand covering her face with her kimono sleeve.

Domon published a series of celebratory send-off scenes of this master and clerk in a special issue of *Nippon* entitled "For the Prosperity of East Asia."

POISED BEFORE HISTORY

What about the line of boys in loincloths caught in the second before the splash: a moment of sheer exuberance in a world of emperor-state fascism? It was taken in the fishing-village resort of Izu. The date is 1936. The next year, on the continent, with the Marco Polo Bridge Incident, full-fledged war with China will begin. Domestically, most signs of dissent have been eliminated. So what about this moment, that is, both the moment and Domon's presentation of it? And of course there's the question of the moment of our viewing. That's why the instant before the splash is charged. We can't reproach the boys for plunging unthinking into the water—for being alive—at that moment. They will undoubtedly be victims in some fashion, and perhaps, depending on their age, victimizers, too.

We can't look at this picture innocently, nor can we think of Domon as innocent.

But what artist is? What adult? Where does adulthood begin?

LOSING TIME

Looking at his pictures, you get the feeling that throughout his adult life Domon rushed from moment to crammed moment until his final stroke.

When I look at my unspeaking grandmother, I tell myself, Know that she is alive now. Take her in with every pore of your body from head to toe.

I usually end up taking a deep breath.

Because lungs are respiratory organs after all, the time passes, empty time. But this is itself a kind of extravagance.

Such extravagance is also an obtuseness, accounting for how we can stand to live day in and day out knowing absolutely that the day will come for each of us when we will no longer spend time.

BOOKMARKS

Domon was a prolific essayist. The essays he wrote in judging contest entries and journal submissions that I've read are unsparing, generous, lucid, never indulging in aesthetic mystification. There is a photo of him judging: he looks like an animal sighting its prey, but a prey as likely to be admired as clawed.

Gazing idly at the book as I awakened, I notice its bookmark dangling gracefully from the white pages and black fabric covers. It's the same kind of flat fabric string used to secure high-quality envelope flaps, obviating the need for glue or tape and inviting multiple reuse. It occurs to me to wonder if all Japanese books in hardcover still come with these markers bound in. (A friend reminds me that when we were children even paperbacks came with such markers; now you get a pile of paper bookmarks.) A quick survey of my table turns up two rather expensive scholarly books without such bookmarks. Maybe their publishers assume these works will be read strategically by readers without any intention of proceeding from cover to cover and therefore needing to keep their place.

BONDS STRANGE AND FAMILIAR

My grandmother is a woman of the north, from Japan's frontierland of Hokkaido. The Clinic Nurse, the Home Helper, everyone remarks on her sturdy bones. Because she ate so much fish, we say, bones and all. She must have gotten more calcium than the rest of us tablet-takers ever will.

Her attachment to her birthplace, Otaru, never weakened. Otaru is now fashionable, a tourist site, the setting of TV dramas. She was never able to return after her family moved to

Tokyo when she was fourteen, meaning that she spent only the earliest fifteen percent of her life there. I don't understand how that sort of attachment works. I imagine Tokyo in the 1920s as an exciting place for a young person, and perhaps it was, but the fragments I have gleaned from her memory are unlovely: muddy streets, cold interiors, tasteless food. Otaru (I am told) was a beautiful port city, her father occasionally prosperous. He had western-style clothing tailored for her and her younger sister in Tokyo and bought her a red sled, the only one in town. Otaru was where she'd been happy. Is that it?

But her relationship with her parents was not what I would describe as warm.

—It would never have occurred to me to answer back to my mother, she told me reprovingly on several occasions. In fact, she added, I never said much of anything at all.

—How about your mother, did she say anything, I asked, guessing that the lecture—not her genre in any case—was over.

—No, she didn't. Parents and children didn't say much to each other in those days.

—Did you like your father?

—Of course, he must have been fond of me. I was the eldest.

My great-grandfather lived long enough for me to have a recollection of him walking the neighborhood in a great black Inverness cape. I know he made and lost more than one fortune. And I have heard that my great-grandmother, herself a renowned beauty, suffered each time they went walking together and he would stop to look at a geisha in a rickshaw passing in the opposite direction.

I know that next to my great-grandparents' house was a tennis court attached to a dormitory for bank employees. One of them proposed marriage to her. Oh, why didn't you, we always said. If you hadn't married Grandfather, we would all have been different.

—Don't be silly, she said. I was only thirteen.

What did the young man see in the beautiful girl? I don't think he ever spoke to her. I don't know that my grandmother could have picked him out from his cohort. So he imagined, or knew, that he wanted this young female beauty, that with her would come a certain kind of life?

I am not being cynical. "A certain kind of life" includes not only material but psychological elements (inner qualities presumed from appearance). Cynicism may be called for, but I have no way to know, and not because the details are lacking. My grandmother's attachment to her birthplace, her unspeaking but probably not uncommunicative relationship with her parents, and her suitor's selection of her suggest a notion of character, and with it of happiness, that is historically removed. But no less (or more) substantial than what I can feel. I envy that capacity for attachment to a face or place as irreducibly unique. Unique—or perhaps rather archetypal, in the irreducible way each of us recalls our childhood or first romance.

Even so, archetypes are produced by geography and social interaction over time—in other words, historically. My grandmother had married, suffered betrayal, raised three children, buried her mother, taken on the care of her youngest brother, run a business, and survived a war by the time she became a grandmother at age thirty-nine. My notion of parent-child love was shaped in girlhood by *Little Women* and my notion of romance in adolescence by *Jane Eyre*. It would not have occurred to me to call love—in English or in translated

Japanese—whatever it was that bound every day of my first eighteen years with hers. And she would not have called it anything. Had we used words, we would have felt ourselves apart in different worlds.

My mother and her foreigner husband—my father—slept in the Western room, as separate from the rest of the house as middle-class Tokyo architecture that had survived the air raids would allow. I slept in the largest tatami-matted room, the Eight-Mat Room, with my two aunts and my grandmother, with whom I shared a futon until I grew too big. It was not so much out of need, this arrangement, but out of that desire to ensure that I be covered at all times, hands and all, in the most frigid season. It must have been suffocating. But what my memory holds is the warmth of the futon in which she told me pitiless folktales, where we listened to the low whistle of boats at dawn in Shinagawa Harbor and the rumble of trains carrying workers who started their days early.

GRANDMAS I

Just as Japanese children today might not intuit the attachment underlying my grandmother's intercourse with her parents, so it is less and less permissible, especially in urban settings, to refer to old women not related to oneself as "grandma." For me it remains a term of affection. To use a term of relationship with a stranger cuts into the chill of contemporary life. (Of course, the chill is also a source of freedom; hence its sometime attraction.)

From My Grandmother's Bedside

I have been lucky to find grandmas on my jogging route. One was on an expensive side street. She was bent ninety degrees at the waist, an unusual sight in the city today. Like the women in a row in Domon Ken's photograph, she must have spent a good part of her adulthood planting, transplanting, caring for, and harvesting rice. She was always out early in the morning, even in the dead of winter, sweeping the already spotless street. She would pause to wave to me, often calling out the standard greeting for sending someone off, whether on an errand, to the workplace, on vacation, to the front. I always turned back before rounding the corner because I knew she would be waiting for a last wave.

Every year I wondered if I'd see her again. She disappeared about the time of my grandmother's first stroke.

Now I have a new grandma, on a more modest street. Most mornings she is cleaning. One morning I am surprised to find her just sitting, no doubt in the hopes of catching a breeze before the sun comes out to roast the day. A cat lies beside her. A red string leads from its collar to her hand. Behind her a structure, or rather a series of structures patched together, extends indefinitely into a luxuriantly neglected garden. With falling slabs of wall and a roof with a fringe of tile in the front but corrugated tin in the back held down with sticks and stones, it looks like an abandoned gingerbread house.

She is mostly toothless and always smiles broadly, bows, and sends me on my way. Today she says sympathetically, Tough job!

She could as well have said, You must be crazy to tire yourself out running when it's going to be deathly hot today. To someone who's obviously used her body in labor throughout life, what I was doing should have been frivolous.

I've never given much thought as to why I like these grandmas. I suppose it's because I've adored my own grandmother, and so I'm predisposed to liking elderly women. On second thought, my grandmother's retiring nature is antithetical to the friendliness of my street grandmas.

I'm grateful for their uncurious warmth. There is nothing in their look that says, Why is this foreigner running through my neighborhood; or even, Is she a foreigner or isn't she. It doesn't matter if the absence of the question is to be explained by failing eyesight or the onset of senility.

I wonder how long I'll keep my grandma with the cat on a string.

NEW GOOD-NIGHT

After the childhood in which I slept beside her or was led hand-in-hand to the doctor's, I rarely touched my grandmother. There was nothing remarkable about that. Even after her first stroke, when her body was opened to all forms of manipulation, she did not invite embrace. Now I sometimes hold her close when turning her over. I put my forehead against her unretreating head. With speech gone, I cherish her weight and the damp warmth of her skin in the dark room.

NIGHT JOURNEY

A professor friend tells me that one in three Tokyoites is from his home region, the snow country of northwestern Japan. The great postwar shift from agriculture to industry profited from massive reserves of young, untrained labor in the countryside. Junior-high-school graduates were sent in by the trainload to take low-paying jobs in Tokyo.

My friend recalls the year he was graduating from junior high. The homeroom teacher asked the students who were going to work in Tokyo to stand up. There were thirteen out of a class of fifty. My friend thinks they were embarrassed. The teacher—an art teacher—asked the standing students one by one whether they wanted to go on to high school. Each answered, Yes. The teacher then addressed the seated members of the class: I want all of you to remember that your classmates want to go on to high school, and that they can't.

On the appointed day of departure, the entire class went to the train station to see the thirteen off. It was a midnight train; the children—that's how young they look in photos—would awake in Tokyo the next morning.

I picture the platform crowded with forms moving in the dark. In March, it would still be cold in the snow country.

Then there is a detail I could not have imagined. The students in the train and the students on the platform held streamers between them as if parting for a great voyage. The moment the streamers tore, they all burst into tears.

My friend says most of his classmates came back in three or four years. They couldn't take life in Tokyo any longer than that. So they came home, where jobs were not awaiting them.

Many, many such partings and dispirited returns must have gone into the economic miracle.

Norma Field

THE IMAGINATION OF TEACHERS

This summer, when everybody is trying to come up with something to say about the fiftieth anniversary, the Japan Teachers' Union, for which "militant" was once a fixed epithet, announced its decision to abandon opposition to raising the Rising Sun and singing the anthem dedicated to the emperor's everlasting reign during school events. It even plans to cooperate with its supreme—indeed, identity-conferring—enemy, the Education Ministry, in an effort to address such intractable problems as student-on-student harassment, *ijime* (for which "bullying" is the standard and extremely inadequate translation).

Weren't there any teachers among the rank and file to suggest a connection between bullying and compulsory use of the flag and anthem? Prewar Japanese were mobilized to join the race of imperialism and to triumph under the sign of the Rising Sun. If the flag and anthem were indeed transformed into symbols everyone would want to support, why was it necessary for the state to mandate their use in schools in the 1990s? Why has the ritually affirmed condition of postwar "peace and prosperity" produced classrooms that are the site of chronic abuse of children by their teachers and other children? Shouldn't it be the task of teachers dedicated to peace education (of all adults, really) to probe the links between the coercive use of national emblems and the costs of an educational system more and more transparently beholden to the needs of the economy—costs choking the humanity of teachers and parents as well as children?

EARTHQUAKES AND EMANCIPATION

On the other hand, there are teachers gathering together in August to think about the lessons of the Great Awaji-Hanshin Earthquake. August marks the six-month anniversary of the earthquake, and there are numerous shows on television about not forgetting the victims—a sure sign that they have already been forgotten.

The teachers recall how, amidst the devastation and chaos of the earthquake, some of the endemic problems of the Japanese educational system disappeared. Schools became evacuation centers, where citizens encamped in gymnasiums for lengthy stays. Once settled, they looked for ways to give something back to the schools. Children who had stayed away from school ("school refusal syndrome") were not only warmly welcomed upon their return but found they had contributions to make. Absent the customary structures of authority, the spontaneous communities of citizens, teachers, and children turned to themselves for decision-making. Middle schools, commonly regarded as the most repressive sector of Japanese schooling (because young adolescents inspire a passion for control in adults the world over?), were transformed overnight by this fortuitous extension of bureaucratic logic: if, given that some students had lost their uniforms along with their homes and therefore all students couldn't be required to wear them, none should be so required.

Normalization has proceeded apace. Uniforms are back. What the teachers were debating was whether there was any way to circumvent total "recovery."

BUS TOUR

There is a bus route I have known for forty years. At first I traveled it on a U.S. Army schoolbus. In those days there was a scary spot under a set of train tracks where Japanese veterans dressed in white and chained to a wall played accordions and thrust out tin cups on a hook.

I may have imagined the chains.

Now those tracks run through one of the youth hot spots of Tokyo. The American base to which the schoolbus carried me disappeared thirty years ago with the Olympics. Glitz sprawls along the route traveled by a commercial bus company.

There's a secret pleasure in taking this bus around seven at night. The boutiques are still lit, the offices humming. On this part of the route, the traffic is just heavy enough to keep the driver's pace comfortable, with pauses here and there that none of the tired passengers seems to mind. A man comes out on the balcony. Why would anyone step out of an air-conditioned room into the steamy city night? He lights up a cigarette. So maybe—remarkably—his office is smoke-free? Or just for the air-conditioned summer? (I remember a friend saying Americans were attempting to abolish death by exiling smokers.) The room he has left behind looks like it's filled with copiers and the usual battery of office equipment. Other white-shirted figures come and go. The man—my man—leans back, takes a deep puff, throws his head back to exhale, then rests his forearms on the railing, cigarette dangling from his right hand. It's tempting to think that he's genuinely relaxed.

Several doors down, at ground level, young women in white ankle-length skirts and empty backpacks deftly inspect racks of clothing identical to what they're wearing. There are also shelves with shirts displayed singly, not in stacks. There were no such shops in space-hungry Tokyo when I was their age.

The light changes, the driver shifts, and I won't know if the one that's fingering the skirt will try it on. Often, as a pedestrian on the night street, I've looked into the lit buses and trains with expressionless men and women hanging from the straps. Now I'm inside the bright moving box, believing that I see without being seen.

Once the bus leaves this neighborhood, even the wider streets are dark, the interiors too obscure to keep me from nodding off. The air-conditioned houses are curtained or shuttered and don't offer the bus rider glimpses of domestic life. At this hour, the most probable scene is dinner being eaten in front of the television. Just before my stop, there's a little burst of light. It comes from a small greengrocer, still open when most other shops have closed. I realize with a start that the light is coming from three light bulbs hanging from an overhead wire. It looks only slightly more permanent than a stall, but it has surely been there for decades.

How bare bulbs illuminate the vigor of exchange: men and women in rubber boots and aprons in fish markets and tofu shops, where water is always running; men in heavy navy aprons with family crests, women in whatever clothes that happen to be practical for hawking fruits and vegetables, tossing coins into baskets suspended from the ceiling. Such is the night view of the stores my grandmother used to patronize by day.

But there are those autumn and winter nights when the bulb burns alone, especially in those shops buried in residential streets.

Loneliness isn't generic. Altogether different is the bare bulb at springtime.

MORNING SLEEP

My mother was still asleep at 6:30 this morning. I'd moved downstairs earlier in the week, when summer began in earnest.

It isn't easy to sleep in the same room as my mother. The radio and desk lamp are next to her pillow, and they go off and on, mostly on, as she awakens through the night. They are traditional equipment for her, but now she's added the air-conditioner remote. She is up and down, touching my grandmother's hands, reading the hygrometer, reading the remote, then shifting from automatic ("neuro") dry to cool, or quick cool, or automatic cool, and then back again. My grandmother's hands come out from under the cover or go back in several times a night.

All of this, not to mention the Combustible or Noncombustible garbage that needs to go out by five A.M.

I pick up the book next to my pillow as noiselessly as I can, wondering if the presence of her daughter, and my potential for speech, have eased her into a rare slumber.

AFTERNOON AWAKENING

The corner tobacco store was the goal of my first solo shopping trip, at age ten. What was I assigned to buy—notebook, matches, tissue, pencils? I don't remember, but I have always bowed to the aging yet changeless proprietor whenever he's minding shop at the little window. His more vigorous wife is seldom stationed there. She probably has other, more demanding things to do. The other day, when I passed by on my bicycle, the window was empty. I had stooped, prepared to bow, so I caught a glimpse of a traditional two-panel curtain swaying in the breeze. In the foreground was a tiny bit of tatami-matted floor, but the curtain suggested a deep, cool recess beyond.

That glimpse of mystery under a relentless sun evoked a memory of awakening free of my mother's vigilant eye. Lying on a child-sized futon of tiny floral print on a sky-blue ground, my eyes opened in the Eight-Mat Room where I slept with my grandmother and my still unmarried aunts at night. In those years the Six-Mat Room-in-the-Back must not yet have been turned over to cast-off utensils, pamphlets, rotting floorboards, and finally mice, so the sliding doors between it and the Eight-Mat Room where I took my naps were left open, giving way to the big window on the far side of the Six-Mat Room. No one had air conditioners in those days. And for that Tokyo was a cooler place.

There was a new high wall between my grandparents' lot and the next-door neighbors'. It was a plain wall of rough wooden slats—this wasn't so long after the war—soaked in creosote. On the neighbor's side of the wall were Japanese cypresses. I remember the dark green of the leaves, the reddish-brown of the preserved wood, the bits of blue sky, and the frenzied cry of cicadas all drenched in sun, in turn blackening the space of the Six-Mat Room between me and the open window.

It was an awakening into a marvelous theater, a theater with a single scene for a single child, suspended in the sensation of elemental urban nature.

DOCTOR'S VISIT

Twice a month, a neighborhood doctor makes a house call. Each time, he changes my grandmother's nasal feeding tube; once a month, he draws blood. My mother then gets a computer printout of my grandmother's health status.

He is gentle with my grandmother and patient with my mother, who is plagued by worries and hypotheses. During my grandmother's most recent convulsion, my mother called him at 6:30 A.M. He advised her to wait it out as usual, to call him back in half an hour. But he called back sooner than that, to make sure the attack had subsided.

This doctor is Taiwanese, but he goes by a Japanese reading of his name. His Japanese is foreign but fluid. How has it been possible for him to have a flourishing practice in our neighborhood, still preserving aspects of a small town within the metropolis? It makes me feel as if either a profound transformation of which I continue to be unaware has taken place or I have been missing some fundamental insight into this society all along.

I know from the experience of friends that we are lucky to know a doctor willing to make house calls. That he is compensated by national health care, that he probably is paid specifically for changing the feeding tube (Japanese doctors are compensated per patient visit, with the consequence, for example, that medication is dispensed in relatively small increments), do not detract from his kindness.

He is willing to take my grandmother seriously. Maybe "willing" is entirely the wrong word, suggesting that he is making a conscious choice in her case. This may be his routine stance toward any patient, from the young and utterly curable to the elderly in steep, unarrestable decline.

He interprets the computer printout for my mother. My mother stores the narrow strips of paper, voluble with information extracted from the blood of a silent person.

GOING TO THE LIBRARY

There are two public ward libraries within walking distance of my grandmother's house. Tokyo is divided into twenty-three administrative wards. My ward has seven libraries. Of the two near me, one is new and gleaming and has videos, CDs, and toys as well as books for check-out. The other is older and cramped but has more volumes. During summer vacation, all the desk space is taken up by young people studying for exams. On weekdays there are also elderly people reading through a variety of newspapers and periodicals. On the other side, mothers chase after young children and read out loud in the hopes of rooting an interest in books. What these devoted mothers don't realize is how disadvantageous a love for reading will be come the adolescent onslaught of entrance examinations.

In my favorite branch there are three computers to tell you about books in print and their availability in the seven branches. If I put in a request for titles held in other libraries, they will be delivered to my branch in a day or two. Readers can also request titles for purchase. There's a big display shelf with books chosen by the staff on specific themes. The end of the War is a favorite summer topic.

My grandmother enjoyed the mysteries that my mother checked out for them both, ten per card at a time.

Upstairs, the library has meeting facilities for local groups and a simple canteen. Right now, a calligraphy class is being conducted for adults and children. The results hang in the spacious lobby downstairs. The children have each written three or four characters related to the season, such as "summer vacation." Now that I think of it, the words chosen for children's calligraphy lessons tend to be stunningly uninspired—prosaic or tiresomely moralizing, usually both. And yet the concentrated effort of the young hand guiding the brush produces a dynamic beauty of form that overwhelms the banality of content.

The adults have received instruction in calligraphy for "practical correspondence," and their handiwork is also displayed.

These public libraries, gymnasiums, art museums, activity centers, and health clinics are manifestations of the decent society potentially signified by postwar "peace and prosperity."

I want especially to remember the mobile bath that visits my grandmother once a week. Three cheerfully professional young people jump from a minitruck at our gate: a nurse, a young man for lifting and carrying, and an assistant. The tub is speedily assembled in the room next to my grandmother's bed and water is drawn from the bathroom. She is gradually lowered into the water on a hammock-like device that can be cranked up and down, soaped from head to toe, soaked again in clean water. Her toenails are trimmed (a hard job for my mother) and her hair blow-dried. In their work, strength and dexterity become tact, and tact, deftness.

Then there is the knowledgeable and encouraging Clinic Nurse who visits once a week to massage, groom, and generally monitor my grandmother's condition. And, most wonderfully, to affirm and reaffirm the labor of the primary caregiver, my mother.

When we family members address my grandmother, we are apt to fall into a prattle. We ask if her legs hurt, promise we are almost done doing whatever bothers her, compliment her unwrinkled skin. She invariably closes her eyes, her remaining gesture of refusal. During the Clinic Nurse's visits, my grandmother's eyes open up. They come alive to talk of the world.

WHISPERS

I had intended the last part of her life to be a time of leisure and comfort. It was to come after the death of her husband. There was no reason to assume his early demise, given the hawk-eyed care of my grandmother, extended not necessarily out of affection but out of an anxiety sustained for so long as to be indistinguishable from devotion. My grandfather's approach to business was, to put it kindly, whimsical; and in any case, the production of matte, monochrome, postcard-sized photos of European and American movie stars on the highest quality paper was an unlikely lifeline for an extended family in the era of Japanese high-growth economics. My grandfather was nine years older than my grandmother, and I counted heavily on that fact to eventually relieve her of his care. But stronger than anything was my need to believe that my grandmother would enjoy an old age that would redeem the rest of her life, and that I could will it into being. I should have known better, of course.

My grandfather did have the decency to die first, less than a year after his wife's stroke. My two aunts struggled over his burial and ended up holding separate ceremonies. My grandmother doesn't know that the man she worried over for nearly seventy years is dead; everyone decided it would be too shocking for her. But she never asked after him, not even before her second stroke, when she had a lot to say. (People laugh at me when they learn that I didn't ask after my dog between the ages of three and twelve. I think my grandmother knew not to ask after her husband.)

My mother lowers her voice to a whisper to tell me about other people's deaths—the cooking teacher on the afternoon TV show, a sumo wrestler, a neighbor. Is it to protect her mother from the distress of such knowledge—the disappearance of those who peopled her life? Or to suspend death itself?

SOAP

Ishigaki Rin writes in an essay about handwashing how laundry in a washtub, allowed to stretch out in rinse water after being twisted and scrubbed and the soap suds wrung out, looks free. It's an essay about the importance of handwork, the importance of not letting the head get too far ahead of the hands.

When I was little I begged to be shown how to wash by hand. I wanted to do something the grown-ups did. It was decided that it wouldn't be a bad thing for me to be doing in summer—the cold water would be refreshing, and there was no risk of my catching cold. So I learned to rinse, changing the water three times, neurotically looking for signs of soap in hiding.

This summer I have been doing more handwashing than in the previous thirty years. It's because I bought some Indian cotton dresses whose dark colors run disastrously. The light, light fabric tempted me in spite of the label: "High-Tech Ethnic."

The dark fabric releases fine eddies of blue into the water. I'm not using a big laundry tub, so the dress can't swim, but Ishigaki's image reminds me of the long washcloth my grandmother used to float in the bathtub before gathering it up to make a giant bubble. It was a way to distract and keep me in the hot water longer than I would otherwise have been willing. Like all children I was fascinated by bubbles, though I wasn't allowed the double pleasure of bubble gum until much later.

We—my cousins, my friend next door, and I—blew soap bubbles with straws. This was quite a different game from the one played by my own children with plastic wands thrust into small plastic bottles of detergent to release a stream of bubbles with a flick of the wrist. I think our first straws were actually made of something strawlike, some form of cellulose, and you had to learn not to suck in and get a mouthful of soapy water. Sometimes we just blew bubbles at each other, snowball fashion. Or we tried to deposit them on plant leaves, where they hovered like Christmas-tree ornaments. We knew most would burst on contact, so the transfer was made with all the caution of which we were capable, and we watched until the fragile walls burst, leaving a circular gleam.

Often, at the end of the day, when we had tired of concocting combinations with sasanqua seeds, pine needles, and other interesting items from the garden, we would come back to our soapy jars and blow the biggest bubbles we could. It was tempting to puncture someone else's bubble, but at this stage in the day it was considered poor form. We usually climbed the Mountain, the camouflaged air-raid shelter in the back of my grandmother's garden. The sunset hour and the effort not to burst our bubbles with haste made us solemn. You were never quite sure how far you dared to blow. If you got it right and let it go just in time, your bubble would ride a current into the darkening sky until you couldn't follow it. You never saw it burst.

DEAD BABY

When the baby girl across the street from us died, I said to my friend next door that we should sweep her soul to heaven. She agreed. It was a summer day, and there were beautifully swirling clouds in the evening sky. My friend and I swept the garden and splashed well water over the parched earth.

I had seen the baby girl a few times with her older sister. I would like to have played with the sister, who was almost my age, but just as I knew I wasn't to ask after my dog, I knew I shouldn't ask to play with the neighborhood children. It was because I wasn't a real Japanese, I thought, but now I don't know whether it was the presence of my father, the moody, oversized American, or his absence after the breakup of the marriage, that caused my family to shrink from the neighborhood.

The baby girl had asthma. The day she died, her mother's sobbing could be heard across the street from the one-room house. Late in the afternoon, a piece of white paper was hung on the bamboo screen over the entrance with two Chinese characters that I found out meant "in the midst of mourning."

That was when I first encountered the character for "mourning." It more directly means "defilement" or "pollution." I had trouble shedding the shape of the character and the black ink from my mind.

My friend and I felt clean and peaceful after the sweeping.

The next day a minibus, not a hearse, came for the funeral party. A tiny coffin of plain wood, to be burnt with the body, was placed in the back. The father and weeping mother did not go. My grandmother explained that this was because it was the duty of children to see to their parents' burial, not the other way around.

ABSENCE

As I approached the spot, I became anxious. I wanted to make sure my grandma was there. Her wooden stool, or more precisely her portable bench, was there. But she was not, which allowed me to see that her house was even more dilapidated than I had grasped from the first furtive glance.

A few feet down the road, her cat was prowling in someone else's yard. It was still wearing a red collar, but with no string attached.

VOICE AND LIMB

—I can't remember what your voice sounds like, Obaachama. It's been so long since you've said anything.

My mother and I were tucking her in after the last tooth-brushing of the day. My mother had seemed so absorbed in the monological routine following my grandmother's second stroke that I was surprised to hear her give voice to such a thought.

Two days later, my mother said to her, I like Mozart. To which her mother responded, I love Mozart.

She came running (though to describe someone as running between these two rooms is absurd) to report Obaachama said, I love Mozart.

This morning the Clinic Nurse came. She rubbed her down, as usual. Then she and the Home Helper struggled to get her in a clean nightgown. My grandmother startled us with a yelp of pain.

Since the second stroke, her right arm is as stiff as the left one. This makes changing her clothes more challenging than ever. It means that it's almost impossible to get her in a nice fresh gown after a hot day without causing her pain. This is also why her right arm, long fastened to her bed railing, is now free. She can no longer move it volitionally. My mother doesn't have to worry about summoning the doctor to reinsert the feeding tube before the scheduled month is up.

(Some patients, our friend the Clinic Nurse once told us, know how to insert their own feeding tubes.)

PEACE AND BANALITY

Peace has no content, no truth, I found myself saying. I wasn't sure where the sentence was going. It's a bit like the opening to *Anna Karenina*—all happy families are alike, every unhappy family is unique. Peace isn't the opposite of war.

That's right. Peace is the world of invisible oppression, said my interviewer, bringing together my thoughts in a way I hadn't managed to.

It's a struggle not to be alienated by the business of fiftieth-anniversary-of-the-end-of-the-war. Peace, peace, peace, peace, peace. The word has been beaten senseless from overuse.

What is the content of peace?

Two high-school girls and a supervisor, also female and a part-timer herself, were shot in the head in a supermarket. Available evidence suggests that it all happened within five minutes. The murderer(s) even failed to break open the safe. A most un-Japanese crime, everyone is saying. (I, too, gasped, thinking, How American. An event so sadly unsurprising for one who lives in Chicago.) Another sign of the changing times, they say. Some say the very brutality suggests that it was a foreigner who committed the crime.

But none of the scanty reports points to a foreign suspect.

As everybody knows, Japan has been a peace nation, a nation for and of peace, for fifty years.

Peace ceases to be banal only when it is threatened. But the moment it's threatened, we lose the capacity to think about it.

BUGS

A small thumping sound at the window. I'm alone in the house with my grandmother. The sound is irregular but insistent. It's coming from the window above me, and I see a small dark form against the paper panels of the sliding doors lining the glass windows. It's probably nothing more than a fly, but its body resounds against the paper as if it were a drumstick and the paper the skin of a drum.

I could get up, open the paper door quickly and then the glass, and hope that it flies out. I am too lazy. But I'm also wary from recent encounters with two cockroaches, one in the kitchen and the other in my grandmother's room. They are prowling at night, scuttling away the instant the light goes on. These are dark, massive creatures, armored cars by comparison with the light brown bugs familiar in northern American cities. I've lost the will for combat that I had when I lived here. And I don't want my mother to know about these fellow in-habitants, because, I tell myself, that would be yet another source of anxiety. But it is more because I dread, am annoyed by, the prospect of adding to her repertoire of ritualized be-havior. So I make a show (to the roaches) of chasing and hope they will somehow do themselves in. More realistically, I buy a boxful of tried-and-tested boric-acid bait on sale. My mother, eagle-eyed as usual about all the wrong things, discovers they are dated to be effective for only another month. I say, The summer will have to end by then.

I listen to the rapping and notice the holes and frayed edges in the paper. The Home Helper is vigorous with the duster, my mother says. We agree this isn't a serious shortcoming.

We've talked about bugs, the Home Helper and I. The kind you collect, not the kind you try to poison. (She is not happy that we won't use more powerful insecticides.) She grew up in the mountainous countryside, so she used to take her children back to shake the trees and capture prized beetles for their summer-vacation projects.

But lately, she says, you can't find any. The dealers get to them first.

CITY OF RAVENS

There are signs posted at two other garbage collection points up the street asking residents not to deposit their garbage before seven A.M. on collection day because of the ravens. I reported this triumphantly to my mother.

—Ravens never get into my garbage, she said with equal confidence.

—You will become the shame of the neighborhood, I pronounced, tacitly acknowledging defeat.

When did ravens take over this city?

Last night, I saw on one of the innumerable nature shows on television vultures swooping to their prey in southern Africa. Neither roach nor raven counts as nature, I suppose. There is, as yet, no technological means of overthrowing the jet-black, every-other-day king of the street.

UNFINISHED ASSIGNMENT: ON HISTORICAL RESPONSIBILITY

The fiftieth anniversary specials here repeatedly show the *Enola Gay* in solitary splendor at the Smithsonian. Interviewed as they leave the exhibit, American after American—thus are people flattened in this context—says, Yes, it was the right thing to drop the bomb, it saved all those American lives. If we had to do it again, if the circumstances were the same, we should do it.

Once in a while, the camera manages to find an American who hesitates before saying, Yes, it was the right thing to do.

For veterans, the quintessential Americans in this context, the past fifty years are the product of nonstop efforts by the United States to achieve peace and order around the world. And rebuild Japan economically, they say pointedly to the Japanese interviewer.

These are the images of Americans circulating on Japanese television around Hiroshima Memorial Day.

I know, and many Japanese know, that there are other kinds of Americans, Americans who have dedicated themselves to the pursuit and propagation of a different view of the war. But it's especially painful on this occasion to encounter Americans whose historical imagination has never, ever been stretched—not even by the knowledge of all the American victims of radiation. And to see mushroom cloud T-shirts and candy bars in the shapes of Little Boy and Fat Man, apparently sold as souvenirs in Los Alamos.

It's thanks to the *Enola Gay* debacle, though, that I realize how one important East Asian view of the bomb coincides with the standard American view. Coincides, that is, insofar as it joins in validation of the bomb for having ended, or at least speeded the ending of, Japanese colonialism.

A citizens' group representing bomb victims in Hiroshima and Nagasaki has mounted an A-bomb exhibit in Seoul, the first such attempt there. Even though the exhibit also focuses on Japanese atrocities on the continent, the bomb-as-deliverer interpretation evidently predominates among Korean viewers. Of course, the reluctance of the Japanese government to officially and sincerely (a necessary contradiction) apologize for the past conduct of the Japanese nation-state and to offer appropriate monetary compensation has blocked the capacity of many Asians to learn about the horrors of nuclear war.

Something else to take in: it has taken fifty years for Japanese citizens to want to appeal the universal threat of nuclear weapons to the fellow Asians whom their country had once colonized. But it is happening.

The American debate has foundered over the number of American lives—even Japanese lives—saved thanks to the bomb. No doubt the bomb contributed to the timing of the end of the war. But any claim about the number of American lives saved is irreducibly hypothetical.

Contesting the saving-the-lives-of-American-boys line is the argument that the U.S.—or Harry S Truman and James

Byrnes, anyway—couldn't give up the opportunity to test the bomb ahead of the Soviets.

This debate commonly entangles two questions: the real reason the U.S. dropped the bomb (why two bombs instead of one being an important subsidiary issue), and whether the bomb(s) in fact caused the war to end when it did. However the first is answered, the question assumes that a decision to use the bomb was indeed made. Another line of reasoning says that arguments of this sort—Truman dropped the bomb to save American lives or to get ahead of the Soviet Union—are obsolete given the structure of modern bureaucracies. Decisions of this scale can no longer be attached to agents (nameable persons) in bureaucratically administered, technological societies. Instead, there is the inexorable force of process.

The American use of the atomic bomb, in other words, offers another set of materials besides the Nazi Holocaust to think about, on the one hand, overlapping but differential kinds of responsibility (of those occupying leadership positions—government, business, military, religious, academic—and of those constituting the category of ordinary citizens), and, on the other, the relationship of human agency to structural causality.

We've had fifty years in which to learn a few things: the lifelong suffering of those irradiated in Hiroshima and Nagasaki, the birth of the second- and third-generation victims (a category still unacknowledged by the government) in Japan, the high incidence of thyroid cancer and other health problems among the young living near Chernobyl, the transformation of life in French Polynesia as a consequence of French testing, the impact of U.S. testing in New Mexico upon inhabitants of the American Southwest, the host of ills reported among those living near nuclear reactors in Washington State or France or England. Then there is the recent (1994) disclosure of radiation experimentation upon a vast range of Americans from the earliest postwar years into the 1960s. We will need to learn much more about these episodes, and we have yet to learn nearly everything about the consequences of Soviet and Chinese testing; but what we do know at least disallows indifference to the use of nuclear power in war or peace.

Americans have avoided and been denied the opportunity to recognize their own nuclear victimization and therefore to incorporate it into the debate about the bombs.

A Polynesian spokesperson from Tahiti says, We are counting heavily on the Japanese, fellow Pacific Islanders as well as nuclear victims, to help us in the struggle against the French decision. To keep the Pacific pacific.

Boycotts are now being attempted by several stores around the country. But most, instead of taking French stock off their shelves, try to get rid of it as quickly as possible, with the result that French goods are better bargains than ever. In any case, the publicity doesn't hurt. A cooperative network argues that Japanese should protest to the French government, not hurt French workers and farmers.

But we know that governments can choose whether to be hurt by words. Loss of money is a more reliable hurt.

Japan pays France to recover a significant amount of plutonium and uranium from its spent fuel rods. Japan has been a faithful ally of the U.S. in the United Nations through the 1970s and early 1980s in opposing restrictions on the possession and testing of nuclear weapons. All the while, Japan has professed the three nonnuclear principles of not making, not storing, and not permitting entry to nuclear weapons.

It has become commonplace to criticize Japan for its victim consciousness, its refusal to take responsibility for its acts of aggression prior to the bombs. But what has been overlooked here, by both the Japanese government and its accusers, is that there might be a responsibility proper to victims as well as to victimizers.

ANNIVERSARY

The official fiftieth anniversary ceremony in Hiroshima is banal—like most official ritual. The address of the mayor, an admirable enough figure, is unexceptionable. Three days later, the anniversary will be observed in Nagasaki. The principal speaker will be the new mayor, who defeated Motoshima Hitoshi four months earlier. Motoshima got a bullet in his lungs for publicly stating that the emperor (Hirohito) had some responsibility for the war. Motoshima campaigned for a fifth term on peace; his rival campaigned on the economy.

People need to work, eat, house, and enjoy themselves. And peace allows people to attend to these needs.

But what is the content of "the economy"? Nagasaki has been and is an armaments town.

Jobs or the environment: this is how the choice is often put in the U.S. Communities in various parts of the world are told that the choice is between nuclear plants and jobs. Native American communities in the southwestern U.S. can choose to bring in money by providing nuclear waste storage or let their young leave in droves until the community vanishes. The Marshall Islands, bombarded by U.S. nuclear testing in the 1950s, have already been subjected to transformations whose effects must be awaited through the staggering half-life of plutonium. Rather than accepting the assessment of U.S. scientists that two of the islands are now habitable again, Marshall Island leaders are proposing that wealthy Asian countries, such as Japan, Taiwan, and South Korea, store their nuclear wastes on those islands. The scheme is opposed not just by international organizations like Greenpeace but by other Pacific Islanders, who are also poor. The Marshallese plan shows that the logic of pitting the economy against the environment is the logic of seeing wealth in injury.

So the choice seems to be between life now and life later. (Though not, of course, for the powerful who manage such logic, nor for the privileged who are their clients, their loved ones, their neighbors.) Does this deserve the name of choice at the end of the twentieth century? So many of us know the answer, know that life can be organized otherwise, and are paralyzed because at the instant that we grasp this knowledge, we are touched by the chill intuition of its impossibility. Or more precisely, we're caught in the tension of knowing what *ought to be done* and that it *ought to be able to be done* in peaceful parliamentary democracies and of knowing that it almost certainly *will not be done.*

After the mayor of Hiroshima's correct speech, a group of children recite a peace pledge: they resolve to overcome differences of language and nationality, to be kind to each other, and to preserve beautiful Planet Earth. We are not meant to picture classroom violence among teachers and students who, after all, speak the same national language.

On an all-night talk show dedicated to the fiftieth anniversary, the emperor system, and the Aum Truth sect, a young and very cool professor, wearing a sport jacket over a white T-shirt, says, I wasn't even born then, I don't feel any responsibility or obligation to apologize; but since Japanese are travelling abroad in large numbers, they need to know something about the history of the War so they won't be embarrassed. We need to teach young Japanese a little history so they'll have some rhetoric at hand if they want to use it.

He's smart and articulate, this professor. The older guests and most of his peers are no match for him. They become agitated. He is unflappable. Much of his analysis makes sense, and you can hear in his narrative line—the dissolution of community and the various fictions invented to disguise it—a comfortable familiarity with Tönnies, Weber, Marx, maybe some Frankfurt School, a lot of French poststructuralism. If kids are violent with each other, it's because human beings who have nothing in common are being forced to spend long hours together. The solution? Hold "events" for them. Circuses enable coexistence.

Where were you when we needed you—at the peak of the cold war?

It's enough to make you want to hug an honest rightwinger.

"PEACE AND PROSPERITY"

This is the season for the litany: because the Japanese people suffered in Hiroshima, Nagasaki, and all sorts of places during the war, they enjoy peace and prosperity today. In the earlier postwar years, it was "peace and democracy."

This exercise in faulty logic—because A follows B, A is caused by B—and bad history enacts an ethical violence. The suffering of people whose cities turned into seas of fire; of children separated from parents during mass evacuation, never to see them again; of student nurses in Okinawa having to dispatch soldiers too weak to move; of the same nurses when they survived long enough to have to kill themselves like other unchosen suicides, the result not only of terror but of the ideology of honor; and yes, of colonists fleeing Manchuria before Soviet troops: these and other limit experiences become unrecognizable as physical pain and mental anguish when transformed into the heroic sacrifice of the Japanese people.

This bit of alchemy adds to the harm done all the victims of Japanese imperialism. That is, the misrecognition of the suffering of Japanese is part and parcel of the nonrecognition of the suffering of Japan's victims. In many cases, those who suffered were both victims and victimizers, as in the case of the Manchurian colonists or the footsoldiers of the Imperial Army. At the same time, we mustn't equate their suffering with that of the Manchurian dispossessed or those tortured and slaughtered in the passage of the Japanese imperial forces.

Of course not, it's easy to say. But it's a tricky process, sorting out victims and victimizers, between and within nations.

Together with the by no means contemptible emancipation provided by refrigerators, washing machines, and flush toilets, the abstract coercion and cruelty accompanying the efficient rhythms of Japanese prosperity are also spreading to successful centers of the former empire. If the flourishing of these centers reproduces Japanese longevity along with fragmenting families, will they also develop mobile baths, visiting nurses, and other, still unimagined social resources?

GUILTY TOUCH

I didn't think I would get caught up in the fifty-year business. It was going to be commercial, predictable, and disheartening: putting paid to the war, memorializing to ensure forgetfulness.

Of course, that was egotistical.

Listening to the news, I find myself stroking my grandmother's shoulder. And I can't help thinking, I touch her because I'm not patient enough to talk to her anymore. And it's for this reason that I write about her.

From My Grandmother's Bedside

PRONOUNS AND THE PERSON

Written Japanese increasingly supplies personal pronouns. Accordingly, one of the criticisms of the June 1995 parliamentary resolution that managed *not* to apologize to Asia is directed at its omission of personal pronouns: it goes to show how Japanese can't take responsibility for anything.

The impulse to litter Japanese sentences with pronouns representing grammatical subject and even various kinds of object is commonly attributed to the influence of English. Whenever I hear arguments about the vagueness of Japanese and the importance of specifying the agent of action and therefore the locus of responsibility, high school memories of learning to read the subject in Latin verbs come back to me. Japanese doesn't work the same way, but the language is rich in resources for indicating agency without resorting to pronoun subject and object. So I wonder what the need for such explicit expression of agency is about. Of course languages respond to various and contradictory forces, but I'm tempted to think of this as a demand for the literal that is the consequence of a generalized bureaucratic sensibility: without a job title and description, appropriate action is no longer discernible.

The mayor of Hiroshima's speech uses verb forms developed to meet the needs of modern objectivity. If translated into English, it would rely heavily on passives, the impersonal *we*, or the construction *it is*. Former Mayor Motoshima's Nagasaki Day speeches used the ordinary polite forms of conversation. It wasn't exactly the same as saying *I, you, we* (nothing is exactly the same between two languages), but there was no doubt that the subject of commitment to the antinuclear cause was the citizenry of Nagasaki, as represented by their mayor; Japanese in general, who were also implicated in appalling acts of destruction on the Asian continent; and finally, all members of humanity committed to the perpetuation of life. I believe the mayor of Hiroshima's speech presumes a similar range of actors, but I don't feel addressed. The enunciating subject implied by his discourse is an omniscient, impersonal repository of morality and science combined; in Motoshima's speech it is citizens, you and me, here and now.

As individuals we're helpless before the prospect of nuclear terror. That's more or less true with the other major forces in our lives. Yet each of us is compelled to live our lives and die our deaths in our own skin—thoroughly penetrated by the world though it is—and so we also need to speak and act from that specificity in the hopes of transcending singleness.

ETHNIC CLOTHING

Maybe it was an impulse for vicarious compensation for my grandmother, who can't be dressed comfortably in anything, that made me buy those three loose-fitting "High-Tech Ethnic" Indian dresses.

I call a friend to report on an interview for which she helped me prepare. She says that that very day she bought an Indian dress and wore it over a T-shirt and found it terribly comfortable. It seemed like the sort of thing I would like, she said; making the purchase must have produced the pleasure of my call.

I have never seen this friend dressed informally or inexpensively, even when we lived close to each other and could, after a fashion, visit casually. So I am touched by this gesture of friendship, made possible by fabric and style sensitive to the wants of the discerning Japanese consumer.

FREE TRADE I

It's not just clothing.

—It's so cheap, this American meat, exclaims my mother happily. It's from Kansas or somewhere.

She proudly displays the filet mignon she bought for the curry I am to make. I could never find anything like it at my supermarket in Chicago. Does this make up for all the Japanese TV sets and camcorders that sell much more cheaply in U.S. discount stores than in Japan?

FREE TRADE II: SEND THE *ENOLA GAY* ONCE MORE

Of course, "off-shore" no longer refers just to U.S. manufacturers moving to Mexico to cut costs. Quite a number of Japanese companies have attempted to counter charges of unfair trading practices by moving part of their production process to the U.S. I have heard that both Japanese and German corporations prefer to locate in the South to minimize the possibility of having to deal with unions. U.S.-based Japanese corporations have also landed in the news for falling afoul of regulations against age, gender, and race discrimination.

On the other hand, the United Steel Workers, demonstrating outside the Japanese Embassy in Washington against the decision of a Japanese company with its U.S. headquarters in Nashville not to rehire striking workers, carried placards calling for the *Enola Gay* to be sent over again.

It surely wouldn't have occurred to them to call for another Auschwitz.

"Hiroshima" and "Auschwitz" have become names for twentieth-century horrors. They represent two very different structures of mass death. The histories to which they refer are both inextricable from the history of the United States. Yet one has been accorded disproportionately less reflection.

So many Americans think the A-bomb was just a bigger bomb, not a different weapon altogether. There's astonishing ignorance of the insidiousness of radiation. If they could only see pictures of those walking corpses with their flesh hanging from them, or the eyes of children awaiting surgery for thyroid cancer in Kiev, or hear those Pacific Islanders who weren't evacuated (deliberately, they now think) for U.S. testing, as well as the American servicemen who watched the tests uninformed of necessary precautions.

FEARFUL SORROW

My grandmother had an avid interest in such matters. It was always an interest that expressed itself as sorrowful sympathy. Those poor people, she would say.

Before her second stroke, she responded from time to time to reports of accidents or natural disasters on the radio with the same sympathy but with an increasingly vivid tinge of fear.

Not long after her first stroke, I was puzzled by her reaction to news of a strike.

—Oh no, oh no. They're making so much trouble.

—Do you think going on strike is a bad thing?

—They're making trouble . . .

This from a woman who was an unswerving socialist from the time she won the vote in 1947.

—I worked all my life, never gave anyone any trouble. Why do I have to suffer like this?

Such candid complaint, so uncharacteristic, could be more unnerving than her physical changes.

My grandmother's dementia wove together her capacity for empathy, her assumption of responsibility for the care of others, and the shock of sudden pain and helplessness into a net of terror that would periodically ensnare her. It was the most cruel form of the anxiety to which her kindness had inevitably bound her, given her usually precarious circumstances.

Dementia made visible the costs of her love that we had preferred not to recognize.

SOUNDS AND GESTURES

Everyone agrees that the cicada are diminished in number this year. Perhaps it was the historic heat of last summer. The larvae, of the kind that spend six years underground before emerging in the seventh year, may not have been able to find enough moisture.

But on this afternoon they are out in force with their song. Song, of course, is metaphoric. Their sounds are produced by rubbing wings. I am too old-fashioned and Japanese, more so than my mother, it turns out, to find them a nuisance. She thinks they make you feel as if you're suffocating in the heat. It's true that stepping into a cascade of cicada song is like walling yourself inside all the summers since time began.

My grandmother has also been producing sounds today. They're like vocalized sighs, one, two, or three notes floated on the still air of her sickroom. Utterances that aren't words. Moan, question, or sigh. Reduced—or perhaps concentrated—commentary on or exchange with the world. Meredith Monk might make music out of it.

If I walk over to her bed, if I call out to her, she will shut her eyes. If they stay open, they will not focus on me.

For my grandmother, the surest way to dignity was sequestration. Don't let anything show, don't let anything be heard.

My poor grandmother. Her family was always erupting.

If only she endured, then the shame would be covered over again, just as her trees screened the house. Payments would be made, weddings held, health recovered, prying eyes averted, and whispers hushed.

So her political convictions subsisted in the depths of a commitment to protective nonassertion. Now she lies mostly in quiet waiting, day in and day out. (But to call it "waiting" is no doubt the logic and therefore self-consolation of the able.) Two years ago, when she was still speaking, she told me she was afraid. Death was in the room, and she needed to escape.

—Mother! she called. Not loudly. She had never been able to shout.

—Here I am! answered my mother, running over and burying her face in her shoulder.

She can't summon any of us any more.

From My Grandmother's Bedside

—At least she doesn't know all the awful things that are going on. She would have gotten sick if she'd seen what they're doing, says my mother, consoling herself that her drama-prone sisters' escalating bad behavior is unknown to their mother.

Well, they have been noisy, but not with their voices. There was the flower pot incident, which ended up with the middle sister announcing to the neighborhood that her brother-in-law was threatening to strangle her. The younger sister adopts the traditional association of salt with purification to her private needs and leaves mounds of salt trailing the path of her uncle, as if my mild, conscientious granduncle were a polluting presence. The middle sister locks my mother out of the house in the dead of winter for disobeying her not only on the garbage question but on the timing for hanging out laundry. Locked out in turn, she calls the police, and flashing lights, patrol cars and bicycles, and above all curious neighbors greet my mother upon her return from getting a month's supply of medication for her mother. The younger sister whispers to the Home Helper that my mother was a prostitute, presumably because she married my GI father; but her punchline is wasted, as the term she uses for "prostitute" is unknown to the Helper, who is a decade or so younger.

My mother was remarkable on that occasion (for of course the Helper dutifully informed her of this episode): I don't want, she said, to put myself in the position of looking down on women who did whatever they could to support themselves and their families back then. She did allow herself a "but," but I'm in no position to begrudge her a qualifier.

My mother is right: My grandmother would not have survived such a display.

WAR AND MEMORY

It began with the stroke and was infinitely exacerbated by the appearance of a will, eight months after my grandfather's death, leaving everything to my younger aunt's son.

The aunts are fighting over the inheritance.

Property is inert, is dead. But it takes on monstrous life in people's heads.

The ferocity of the battle being waged by my aunts makes me think that the house and garden ooze bitterness from every childhood slight, every glance cast at one and not the other, every bout of illness granted one and not the other as the occasion of anxious devotion. My mother is the daughter who failed in marriage, who has lived virtually all her life with her mother and father. Sometimes I think she is unforgiven precisely because she failed in marriage and was therefore able to stay with their mother.

(In the misery of battle I'm apt to forget the whole of postwar history, which also shaped the sisters' lives so that we are where we are today.)

Today I join her in the first morning rituals of my grandmother's daily care.

—See if you can get the handkerchief out of her left hand, says my mother.

My grandmother has had a fresh handkerchief inserted in each hand since her stroke, to absorb the sweat from her palms. Before the second stroke, the handkerchief in her paralyzed left hand was woven in and out of her fingers. That's too hard now. I try to unlock her knuckles. She clenches tighter. I don't want to be wrestling her. She clamps her jaws when my mother or the Clinic Nurse tries to brush her teeth. (Remember, Obaachama, three minutes after meals, you always said, . . . it's all over if you wait longer than that.) It's involuntary, I know, but watching her un-speaking face I can't help thinking that this, too, is seques-tration, unprotesting, undemanding, utterly in keeping with her character.

CLIMATE CONTROL

Ghost stories are supposed to cool you off in the summer heat. You sweat with terror, and then you're cool.

This time of year my mother loves to watch actors' rendi-tions of supernatural experiences allegedly sent in by the view-ers of noontime television.

Ghosts are good for more than cooling you off. Even if this isn't a psychologizing society, the expert analysis of viewer ex-perience draws on such categories as jealousy, unfulfilled de-sire, or mourning. It connects the present with the past, but the lesson of ghost stories is always that the past must be kept separate from the present. It's preferable to appease ghosts and send them back. If you can't do that, run away.

Maybe this is mature.

HORROR

More horrifying than any ghost story is a parent's inconti-nence.

My aunts do not change my grandmother.

And they never come around to see her in the mobile bath, says the Home Helper.

My grandmother's terror before death and our horror before her incapacity merge without producing a common courage.

GRANDMAS II

I passed two grandmas this morning. Both must have been lifelong city women, for their backs were absolutely straight. One was a new-style grandma: bold, sophisticated print blouse and trim beige skirt. She was not trying to look young, but she had also refused clothing that labeled itself as strictly functional, for those who shouldn't call attention to themselves. Her concession to age was nylon anklets worn with casual sandals. No sunshade. She must have thought it was early enough in the day.

The other grandma was walking in the opposite direction. She was using a large, dark green umbrella as a sunshade. Her blouse was a shapeless light grey, her skirt another noncolor. She had grey socks with split toes for traditional sandals with woven straw lining, cool to the sole in summer. Her legs were two dry sticks growing out of the socks. She used a cane.

To watch her progress, therefore, was to follow three sticks advancing in rhythmic harmony. I used to think—smugly— how youthful my grandmother was by comparison to such women, even though she was probably much older. After her first stroke, I became envious of their mobility. Now I simply appreciate the mobility of any elderly person.

My grandmother's appearance probably did not invite address or reference as "grandma." The new-style old woman's might not, either. The sartorial conquest of age is an achieve-ment of modernity increasingly visible in Japan as elsewhere. But there's also a current, expensive counterpart to the three-legged grandma's dress. It's the dark kimono of expensive fab-ric, trimmed with fine accessories. It, too, says "I am old, I ought not call attention to myself," but at the same time, it would probably ward off the anonymous call of "grandma."

It's not so much, or mostly, that people think abstractly, on principle, about removing gender or age discrimination. Changing fashion prompts such thinking, secretly greasing the wheels of rationalization.

My grandma with the red-stringed kitty has reappeared. The past two times I've seen her, she's had her hair up in an old-fashioned, oddly elegant style, no doubt because of the heat. It's pleasantly incongruous with her sunburnt wrinkles, plaid shirt, and navy sweat pants.

AUNTIE

I hadn't seen her in fifteen years. She is my grandmother's only sister, two years younger. After them came three boys. When they were little, in the teens of this century, they were dressed in exquisite white dresses and bonnets and photographed with a doll carriage. They were themselves solemn, gorgeous dolls.

I remember her as the rich relative, though I don't think that was always justified. She was always elegant, even in the hard postwar years when she worked for my grandparents. Her voice was clear and somehow musical, and her hair tightly curled. No stranger would have dreamed of calling her "grandma."

She was plump, too, unlike my grandmother. But now she has lost over half her body weight. She has colon cancer. She has not been told this diagnosis.

She is more beautiful than in her prime. Her hair is now straight and grey. Her eyes hold you steadily, at times quizzically, though not unkindly.

She wants to know about her older sister, whom she hasn't been able to visit in months. I hadn't known how deeply she cared.

Earlier, on the telephone, I almost told her how little my grandmother was speaking when I caught my mother's frantic signals. Just as my grandmother has not been told of her husband's death, so Auntie is not to hear about her sister's second stroke because she herself has just undergone surgery. But my middle aunt has spilled the news, apparently in order to complain about my mother, so now Auntie wants to know just how many words her sister uses and how often.

I am clumsy. Caught in an initial lie, I add word upon word, hoping to neutralize, shift, disguise. Auntie contemplates my collapsing edifice with detachment, perhaps even a touch of amusement. My grandmother always said she was tough, a tomboy. When they were girls on their way home from afternoon play, the boys used to block her path but not my grandmother's.

She and her family went out to Manchuria when it was part of the empire. They manage to look stylish even in the photos taken after their return upon Japan's defeat. A son died of bone cancer not long after. When Auntie's husband died, my grandmother took me to visit her. They lived in a two-room house then, one room on top of the other. I wondered why I was taken along. I was too much a child to understand the child function of providing relief from the gravity of the adult world. I also remember being reluctant to go to a house where someone had so recently died. Who knew what might be lurking there? What greeted me was the peculiar effect of a presence that had been swept away, leaving its trace in the emptiness that was not the same as bareness. Though there was that, too. I remember thinking, This must be what grown-ups call loneliness.

I walked out under the starry night sky of November with my grandmother.

After that, Auntie's life gradually became much more comfortable, and my grandmother's less so. They continued to care for each other in a way I lacked the eyes and wit to recognize, perhaps because of a stunted imagination about the effects of material privilege.

She is happy to see me now. As are the two of her three daughters who are with her today. They welcome me with unquestioning intimacy. I worried about the meeting because I wasn't to let her know how much her sister had declined. That requirement turned out not to hold, exactly, but I was still bound to the principle of not causing anxiety.

She wonders how long it will take her to get out of the house again. She's managing to take her meals sitting up at the table.

My heart isn't in the deception. In fact, it's too simple to call it deception, because I think she knows. Each of us knows the other knows, but neither of us is free to acknowledge it.

She wants to see my children's pictures, and she wants me to meet her great-grandson. She wants me to explain why her sister's three daughters can't get along and help each other out, unlike her three girls, even though—her tone is keenly analytical—their circumstances are quite disparate as well. I begin by suggesting that the middle sister has long suffered from a sort of autism.

—What?

—Autism. Not literally, of course, because she's an adult.

—Well, we can't call it autism then, can we.

—No, I suppose not.

I don't want to embark on a discussion of the struggle for property. It would make both of us miserable, even more miserable, I think, than to acknowledge the approach of death.

I'm casting about for another kind of story when a nurse comes to administer an injection. Auntie has been told it bolsters her immune system. It is in fact a still unrecognized treatment for cancer.

Having just rediscovered Auntie, I'm not ready to part with her.

USEFUL MOBILITY

There are walkers here too, for the elderly who are unsteady on their feet. They look like baby carriages, and they were surely inspired by the sight of grandmas pushing their grandchildren.

These walkers have pouches in the back in addition to the main covered waterproof compartment. Thus, the grandmas who push them can do a little shopping on their daily outings.

I have never seen men with these walkers. Elderly infirm men, when they appear in public, use canes. They are not as long-lived as women, but is it also that they are less capable in old age? Or that society cannot imagine a use for them?

The American walker looks so unwieldy, like a portable jungle gym. Maybe that makes it safer, but it fails to anticipate useful activity beyond locomotion.

POSTWAR HISTORY I

There is a flurry of activity across the street. It's the dust that must have subliminally made me choose the word "flurry." Three little factories had stood side by side, so built into each other that I for one hadn't realized they were discrete entities until the middle one was torn down this spring.

Now, an outlandishly tall, whitish A-frame is going up in place of the dark wooden structure in which red sparks and blue flames had flown night and day, year after year. This morning I saw that sod was being laid from the street to the front door. On either side still stand the "town factories" that supported the economic miracle. One of them has been covered with hideous blue plastic shades for years, no doubt because bamboo isn't as lasting. The other one looks like a jigsaw puzzle whose pieces were never meant to fit together. The owners of the A-frame had wanted to remove this structure and its occupants, but the occupants had prevailed in court. They are the family of the dead baby of my childhood. Now there are baby grandchildren.

Checking with my mother, I confirm that the parent generation of the owners of the A-frame, before operating a factory, had sold eggs from their house. That was when the road separating their house from ours was still unpaved and traveled by horses on occasion. For a number of years, probably until open ditches were covered for the Tokyo Olympics, the road would flood every time the pool was drained at the school "up" from us. Here comes the pool! a child would shout, and the next instant, just like a real flood, the water would come rushing down and children would jump in, whooping with pleasure. A month later, the same road became one of the principal routes of the autumn festival. Portable shrines for both children and adults followed by huge drum floats pulled by children passed our house from late morning through the afternoon. Each set of three was preceded by harbingers in the form of grizzled men—the elders of the district associated with a given shrine—who walked with clanging staffs. More often than not, it was my mother who would shout, Here they come! and we would rush to the western room facing the road and peek from behind the lace curtains. I imagined myself among the cotton-kimono-clad girls pulling the drum, but this was something else I knew not to ask for.

Such understanding added to the width of the road between our house and the egg store, so the crossing one summer day survives in my memory.

Was it the whim of one or the other unmarried aunt? Dressed in ruffled yellow organdy and carrying a small but sturdy woven basket, I was walked across the street to ask for the requisite number of eggs. The mistress of the house, who has long since died and is therefore unable to occupy the outlandish A-frame, counted out the eggs for me and placed them carefully in my basket.

I was adored, indeed caressed, without a single touch.

FORBIDDEN WORDS

That had nothing to do with me individually. I embodied Child Dressed Up, solemnly playing at the task of going-on-an-errand. For that I was gazed upon with affection and pleasure. The word would be an old-fashioned one, *mederu*, in which the act of gazing is itself the act of loving and appreciating, whether the object is an instantiation of nature's beauty, such as a cherry blossom, or of a quality, such as loyalty. The object of attention ceases to be mere object, but it is precisely not personalized. Insofar as I did not embody Japanese Child, I must have been construed as Western Doll. There was nothing doll-like about my plump, unalert features, but that did not matter.

The cultivation of essences, the belief that they exist, whether in nature or as artifact or character, is seductive and constraining. Drawn to its deployment in poetry and painting and performance, I long failed to recognize its power to stunt and deceive. Feeling betrayed, I became vigilant, in part out of shame over my blindness, and forbade myself pleasure in things announcing themselves as distinctly Japanese. This was the prison I fancied Domon Ken might rescue me from. Now, I find words like *mederu* straying into my head. I roll them on my tongue, still unvoiced.

GROWN-UP HOMECOMING

The waves of reconciliation lapping at my mind, reattaching me to place and the time captured therein, toss up other words: *amaashi,* the feet of rain, for the passage of rain, typically swift, or simply its appearance; *igokochi,* the quality of heart or mind of being-in-a-place, as in comfort on a sunny verandah in spring or discomfort in a new job; *hirusagari,* the time after noon, the most intense part of daylight; *oyado,* dwelling, with diminutive *o,* as in *suzume-no-oyado,* the sparrow's little house, the house inviting to sparrows, the name given an old farmhouse in a bamboo grove turned into a municipal park near my grandmother's.

Every language has words that can only be described in, not translated into, another language. Maybe all words are untranslatable, but some are more so than others.

(In the meantime, the entire world is being anglicized.)

I throw up my hands and decide to go to a Kabuki performance for the first time in a dozen years. The cheapest seats are twice what they used to be, even putting aside the exchange rate.

From the beating of the sticks announcing curtain time as the running figure pulls back the curtain striped in dark green and black and adzuki brown, I can hardly sit in my seat. I'm not a sophisticated viewer; I just can't resist the rhythms of drums, sticks, *samisen,* audience calls, frozen poses. I adore being able to nibble and sip with my eye on the stage. Best of all, I have a friend to nibble with.

The first play in the evening's program is set at what is conventionally known as the beginning of Japanese modernity, the eve of the Meiji Restoration (1868). The repartee between two powerful men over the fate of the city of Edo, about to become Tokyo, and the last Shogun, Keiki, is classic, with extravagant exchange of swagger and empathy. Appeal to the threat of foreign—western—forces wins the day.

Can this selection be accidental, during the summer of the fiftieth anniversary? The play was first performed in 1933. My friend reminds me that was the year Japan, barraged with criticism for its conquest of Manchuria, withdrew from the League of Nations.

And still I loved the evening.

SWEETS

My favorite shopping takes place in the arcade of the neighborhood where my grandparents lived in a rented house with their daughters and employees before they evacuated to the countryside late in the War. Most of the neighborhood was leveled by incendiary bombing, and even the place names have changed.

This summer, a new Japanese confectionery shop appeared. There were already two others. The first is not too proud to have a restaurant that my grandmother enjoyed with her great-grandchildren. In addition to traditional Japanese sweets and ices in the summer, it serves a variety of Chinese noodles, including the "Power Noodles" that were once my son's favorite, loaded with vegetables and meat topped off with two Japanese rice cakes in a flourish of culinary miscegenation. The second shop is elegant. I will always remember it because it features sweets to display with the court dolls on Girls' Day, March 3. You can bring in the miniature bowls, plates, and baskets year after year and have them refilled. The new store is the most expensive, but on weekends and holidays it sets up stands at the front of the store for selling popularly priced items such as small dumplings wrapped in bamboo leaves and green-tea flavored dumplings in cold adzuki-bean sauce.

One evening, inquiring about the bamboo-wrapped sweets as the stands were being cleared away gave me the chance to step inside the store and glimpse its regular offerings, such as *yōkaten*, Distant Flowers in the Heavens; *setsureika*, Flowering Snowy Peak; or *shun'yūroku*, Fruits of Spring Outing. The lyrical dignity of these sinicized names is impossible to render in English, but they designate variously layered combinations of sweet pastes, whether of chestnut, figs, adzuki beans, or yam. I promised myself I will find an occasion to make a present of one.

CIVILIZATION

It is now possible to buy not only socks and lingerie but pencils, erasers, and telephones that are labeled "anti-germ processed." You might think that practically anything that touched the human flesh can now be so "processed," but no doubt more specific patterns would emerge from a thorough survey. Initially obvious categories are things handled by children and things that touch the mouth or feet.

This phenomenon challenges the view that people are insensitive to the dangers of radiation, for example, because it is invisible. A television commercial uses electron microscopy to demonstrate the difference between unprocessed and anti-germ processed socks each worn for one day.

In this hyper-thin society, the customs office at the Tokyo International Airport is plagued by mountains of thinning soap brought back by women travelers to China. It's not un-available here, but it is classified as medication and is therefore subject to regulation, so it comes a lot cheaper in China. What a brilliant product this is, reinforcing the appeal to the fetish of thinness by invoking the even more basic fetish of cleanli-ness, making it seem as easy (and essential) to shed weight as to wash off dirt.

The odorless, fatless, dirt-free body dreams of an unconta-minated environment, a dream thriving in symbiosis with air, water, and ground pollution. In retrospect it becomes obvious that this was the perfect setting for a massive outbreak of *E. coli* (type 0157) in the summer of 1996, leading to the collapse of the white radish sprout market, the installation of hot air cur-tains in school cafeterias, and discrimination against children and other victims of the disease.

We could laugh—and weep—over the fragility of advanced capitalist societies.

AND BOMBS

Weep I do over my mother's shattered domination. In my bolder moments of childhood vulnerability, I classified her scoldings as atomic or hydrogen bombs.

LAUNDRY

If you were to meet my mother, among the last words you would associate with her might be *calm*. The weather forecast calls for rain. Never mind how often the National Meteorological Agency is wrong: she is out on the verandah, tearing the laundry off its pins, running upstairs to hang it up, stubbing her toes in the process.

This morning I got up first for once and brought in the laundry. It had rained for at most five minutes. There are so many kinds of laundry hangers here for differently cramped spaces: circular, rectangular, large, medium, small, tiered, collapsible. They are plastic frames with clothespins hanging from them. Some of my mother's are antique enough to be all metal and entirely rusted. The pins keep falling off, and my mother reattaches them with bits of wire found who knows where. (She also has a habit of clipping the pins to her blouse, sometimes an army paralleling the buttons.) Even the plastic hangers are discolored and deformed, perhaps from being hung over the stove in winter. Don't let a billowing sheet catch fire one of these days.

My mother fulfills each of her responsibilities conscientiously, or rather, ardently, whether it's reattaching clothespins, clipping newspaper articles for me, putting out the garbage, or finding a telephone number. Everything is done as the thought occurs. This makes her an exhausting companion.

Since my grandmother's stroke, she has of course had to take charge of the finances. We have had several bouts of panic this summer because she could not find the bank receipts for major payments. She is unaccustomed to dealing with computer records; filing is a novel concept. I become irritable out of anxiety. My grandmother always kept something called "the red *furoshiki*," a little bundle secured in a red-faded-to-orange wrap, in one of the bedding closets. In case of fire or earthquake, that was the one thing to be taken out. That, and her mind, were her files.

Watching my stricken mother pleading with bank clerks over the telephone, I recall the story of an acquaintance's mother in the U.S. She was certainly of average intelligence, the daughter conceded, but when she took a test in the hopes of becoming a postal clerk, she couldn't understand how to use the computerized answer sheet—the kind for which you're to bring No. 2 pencils in order to Record All Your Answers on the Answer Sheet Only. That was thirty years ago.

My diligent mother is always calling offices to find out if she's made one or another payment. She seems not to be persuaded by my view that where payment is concerned, *they* will get in touch with you.

ONE A.M.

Last night I changed her by myself. My mother was sound asleep and did not jump up, as she usually does. It changed the nature of the task to feel that my grandmother's comfort was, for the moment, entirely in my hands.

Of course, I've taken care of her by myself many times in the past three years. But it was different when she was speaking.

I tuck a pillow under her back to shift her weight. For three-and-a-half years, approximately every three hours, my mother has done this in order to ward off bedsores. It has become progressively harder for her to do this because my grand-mother has gained weight from her excellent liquid diet while my mother has thinned. Even when both were healthy, my grandmother was the taller. (My mother, the oldest of the three sisters, is the smallest. The common family understanding is that she entered adolescence just as food became scarce. Or, alternatively, that she was picky about food and never ate enough small fish, whose bones were an important source of calcium in the prewar diet.)

Since the second stroke, it's hard to tell if my grandmother's body has in fact been turned. Neither leg will straighten, and however she's positioned she ends up facing her right. If you tuck the pillow in deeper just to reassure yourself that you've done the job, her face is drawn in pain from having all the weight rest on one shoulder. So you have to tilt that shoulder and redistribute the weight to her back.

Her face relaxes. I wish her good-night, turn out the over-head light. The dim alcove light is still on. Her eyes stay open in the dead of night.

POSTWAR HISTORY II

For many, many years, afternoon television in Japan was one everlasting Hollywood movie dubbed into Japanese. All the voices were the same. And the Japanese voice actors and actresses didn't sound like any living Japanese men or women. When did Hollywood retreat from the afternoon household?

To be replaced by talk shows. Every funeral and wedding of note in the archipelago is covered. The dismissal of Hollywood has been achieved by exploiting the fascination with accidents and crime in a society that is never safe enough. 1995 is a boom year. The Great Awaji-Hanshin Earthquake in January has been followed by the endless exploits of the Aum Truth sect. The country may be cynically indifferent to national politics, but national unity is reknit each day through the afternoon talk show, at least for the homebound females of the citizenry.

The genre of the Japanese talk show has several variations, however, and their offerings are not limited to the staple of scandal and accident. This isn't called an information society for nothing. Like news programs, health, cooking, and diet shows use statistics, charts, and diagrams to a degree unimaginable in the U.S. They also let you see the difference between the perfect tuna cells in *sashimi* slices cut with properly sharpened knives and the mangled cells that survive unsharpened knives. You learn that if you lie in a coffinlike machine that can measure the precise amount of your body fat, you might discover that even if you haven't gained a kilo you'd better start worrying, because a greater portion of your body weight consists of fat than a year ago. Wait a couple of hours and you might pick up techniques for treating all manner of bodily ills through the application of five-, ten-, or hundred-yen coins at acupressure points.

But "pick up" is not quite right, for despite the consistently upbeat tone and the exasperating delight emitted by commercials, there is the sense that there are lessons to be learned. Indeed, you may feel as if you ought to be taking notes. You can't—I can't—remember which coins to put on what part of the soles of the feet, and watching the program, you feel you will want to remember.

My mother's favorite weekday noon show has a history spot featuring some event or process or person with a significant date falling on that day. During the anniversary summer many of the items are, not surprisingly, connected to the War. It turns out that August 11 is the day the elephant Indira arrived as a gift to the Ueno Zoo in Tokyo. Zoo animals, too, suffered in the war. The fate of the elephants at Ueno is especially well known: they were killed by grieving attendants—so the story goes—to prevent a stampede in the event of bombing. (No doubt other large animals were as well, but their stories must have been less promising for illustrated circulation.) Indira was presented by Prime Minister Jawaharlal Nehru of India in response to a request from war-saddened schoolchildren in Tokyo. Indira, of course, was named after his daughter, Indira Gandhi.

I thought I remembered the story of Indira's coming, but that turns out to be chronologically impossible. What is likely is that I heard radio reports of Nehru's reunion with Indira in 1957.

The images of Indira's arrival in 1949 are stunning. She walked from the port of disembarkation to the zoo, where she immediately became queen of the realm. She traveled by train and was greeted by cheering, flag-waving crowds. One of her attendants recalls how unhappy she was, at least initially, with the commotion. She refused to step out of the freight car. And elephants, when upset, apparently develop diarrhea. She soiled the attendant's fanciest uniform before the festivities had even gotten underway.

All over Japan, in the days when people were still hungry, they brought offerings—typically sweet potatoes—for Indira. (Domon Ken photographed a roasted-sweet-potato thief in Ueno Park in Tokyo of 1950). Her attendants enjoyed what she could not eat. No media star could have competed with Indira, except perhaps the newly democratized emperor, surveying the devastated land and inspiring the exhausted people. Indeed, with the flags and throngs, Indira's procession properly recalls an imperial progress.

Is it testimony to the power of modernity that people think to wave national flags at an elephant?

Then there is the specific historical relationship between Japan and India, as manifested in Chandra Bose's wartime movement to support the putative Japanese goal of liberating Asia from Western imperialism or Radhabinod Pal's solitary refusal to join in the guilty votes in the Tokyo Trial (the International Military Tribunal of the Far East).

Was it only children who were more cheered by Indira the elephant than Hirohito the human emperor?

HAIRCUT IN BED

Since her stroke, my grandmother has had her hair cut at least once a year. My mother gets coupons from the ward office, and she can choose from a number of beauticians or barbers who have registered to give home haircuts and be publicly re-imbursed. She chose one out of the book. A lady barber, tall, striking, with—exceptional for a contemporary Japanese woman—undyed grey hair came with a basket of tools.

The first two years, my grandmother was strong enough to be seated in her wheelchair for the occasion. Wrapped in a bar-ber's apron, she sat quietly but with curious eyes wide open. The barber was swift and skilled. Thank goodness. We knew, or thought we knew, how tiring it was for her to be sitting up, and the heat was an added burden. For the first time in her life, my grandmother got an old-fashioned old lady's haircut. She wouldn't have liked it had she still had those categories.

This morning, she stays in bed for her haircut. The barber's apron goes more over her bed than her body. To do the back of her head, the barber suggests we lower the incline of her hospital bed and prop a big pillow behind her back. Then my mother holds her head while the barber snips away. Unusually for these days, my grandmother keeps her eyes open.

In her girlhood she had knee-length hair, so thick as to be bothersome, she said. She belonged to the early wave of women who bobbed their hair and wore dresses and skirts. She found it more comfortable, and she probably liked the look. Beyond the physical ease, though, it did little in the way of emancipation. She used to say, watching talk shows in the late 1970s and early 1980s in which women who had left their families were found by television staff and made to listen to the appeals of their bedraggled husbands and tearful children, How lucky women are nowadays to be able to find a job somewhere. Of course, jobs such as café-waitressing existed in her day, but she was too middle class to know how to find them.

I don't remember my grandmother going to beauty parlors. She didn't much care for the results she saw on other women's heads, and she didn't like the expense. So my mother trimmed her hair. She had a few nice clothes for unavoidable occasions, but they were almost always consigned to closets, drawers, tea chests, and mothballs. In summer, she wore simple dark cotton dresses or an open-collared blouse and plain skirt. In winter she added layers of wool. The top layer, regardless of season, was an apron. When I was little she wore the old-fashioned white aprons with sleeves known as *kappōgi*, but as she grew older, she switched to simple aprons tied at the waist. I eventually learned her preference and bought her large all-cotton ones with big pockets to hold the miscellaneous useful things she was apt to accumulate in the course of a day—rubber bands, safety pins, tissue. She eschewed expense but was always fastidious, in contrast to my mother, who shows a dismaying tendency to wear anything that will cover her as long as it has sleeves and a collar.

The haircut in bed: I wonder if my grandmother could experience as pleasure the sensation of having her hair fingered again. And whether the memory of how beauticians made women look not themselves was triggered by the sensation, giving her that fine look of concentration.

Afterwards, we had to change her nightgown, pads, and sheets. Neither my mother, the Home Helper, nor I could figure out the optimal order for executing this task so as to minimize hair scattering. We decided on one way, then reversed ourselves. It turned out not to matter because the lady barber had done such an expert job. As usual, my mother immediately tackled the new mountain of laundry. I tugged at my grandmother's firmly bent left leg and put the foot on the red bean-bag pillow, stretched the somewhat looser right leg, shoved a pillow between her knees so as to keep her legs from becoming altogether inseparable, tucked another pillow behind her back, then raised the head and foot sections of her bed. The Home Helper covered her with the terry-cloth blanket, leaving her hands out so they wouldn't get too steamy.

Looking the picture of clean comfort, she fell into a deep sleep. Even a haircut in bed can be exhausting.

AFTERNOON BEFORE FALL

There is a word in Japanese, *komorebi*, that might literally be translated "spilling sun." It refers to sunlight filtered through leaves.

My grandmother used to worry, after the camouflaged air-raid shelter was dismantled and new trees and shrubs planted, that not enough sunlight came through for the annuals and perennials she couldn't resist planting, watering, and weeding even though all her garden space had been taken up.

The result of all this planting is constantly varying patterns of "spilling sun." On this August afternoon, her garden is a symphony of lespedeza grass, weeping cherry, bouquets of lavender crepe myrtle and phlox, and laundry: the nightgown, towels, and sheets from the haircut. Caught in the wind, they dance in a sunlight already anticipating autumn.

From My Grandmother's Bedside

DIALOGUE

It's not just me. My grandmother shuts her eyes as soon as any of us approaches. I was about to write, as soon as she notices we are approaching, but it occurs to me that I can't assume she *notices* in any usual sense. Her attention, operating at subterranean depths, might be all the keener for the loss of intermediate interpretive filters.

She doesn't want to be bothered, says my mother affectionately. Are you playing Mr. Badger, asks the Home Helper, introducing me to a gentle version of the expression, "badger-sleep," meaning pretended sleep, of which I was often accused during the years when naps were a daily requirement.

At other times, when fluttering notes come from my grandmother's bed, my mother rushes over to ask if she's all right, if she wants anything. Lately, though, I've noticed that instead of running to her bedside, especially at night, my mother floats back a sound, at core a Yes, or an Obaachama, but a sound more and more losing its verbal contours and growing melodious.

My mother has always viewed with foreboding the onset of fall. Now, I picture to myself the two old women lying side by side and floating their messages to each other through the long night.

KINDS OF TALK I

My mother had a special vocabulary for the series of cats we had, beginning with Mimi, who evacuated to the countryside with the family in the last year of the War, and ending with

Chiro, the eternal little-boy cat hit by a car when I was sixteen and away on a school trip. She invented names and jingles with her own onomatopoeia for wiping their feet (they were kept tied up in the house, allowed to roam freely outside, then bounced and scraped on newspaper for a thorough paw-cleaning), feeding them, or simply talking to them.

Chiro has been dead thirty years. Some of my mother's cat vocabulary has resurfaced in the care of my grandmother.

—She's not a cat, I'll say.

But cat-talk is preferable to baby-talk. Once, only once, I said,

—She isn't a baby.

I didn't get the edge out of my tone.

—She might as well be.

Was there a touch of sharpness in her tone? She adored the cats, she adores me, she adores her mother.

I try to think: maybe a radical shift of vocabulary—a species shift, as it were—is one way to be tactful with an adult human being who can no longer perform the defining functions of grown personhood. Baby-talk makes caresses possible where none would otherwise be ventured.

But if there is tact, it's also exercised for our own need to keep at bay our fearful dismay over the disintegration of the one who had held the world together for us.

KINDS OF TALK II

But I can hardly stand it. I barely contain myself listening to my aunt next door speak to her mother, baby talk combined with repetitions of areyouwell areyouwell areyouwell Obaachama?

Ofcourseshesnot . . . ittiresheroutjusttolistentoyou.

I know each of us is frantic to repay her particular debt to the poor woman at our center. This makes us more ungenerous with each other than we have ever been in our lives. It would be enough to kill the object of our love were she not protected by illness.

The other day, my aunt put on Bach's Air on the G String. She says she knows her mother's favorite colors and music. That time I muttered, ostensibly to my mother and granduncle sitting in the next room, That's great music if you're dying, or better yet, dead.

She also places her hand on her mother's head and prays over her. According to what creed I don't know. She's undergone a few conversions, and I've lost track.

—Why doesn't Obaachama ever answer? she asks.

My mother says she's always asking. This aunt holds my mother responsible for both strokes, the first because she did not force her to go to the doctor to have her blood pressure taken when my aunt thought she looked unwell, the second because she let her be bathed in the mobile bath even though she was running a low fever.

Those are the stated reasons.

KINDS OF TALK III

It wasn't always like this.

After the first stroke, after the two long weeks of coma, she began to talk again. It wasn't the way she had talked for the previous eighty years of her life. My poststroke grandmother was an almost new person. She seemed to be discovering words as a direct expression of feeling for the first time.

—If you hurry up and get well, Obaachama, you can tend to your garden again.

—Don't want to get well.

I don't have an answer for this. Then I try,

—What if you didn't have to do anything? Would it be all right to get well then?

Long pause.

—Maybe.

—The tulip tree has been spectacular this year. And the flowering quince looks like it's going to be beautiful, too.

—No need for them to blossom like that.

Just as shocking as her candor is her use of informal verb endings with strangers, such as nurses. Then again, she can surprise with formal greetings—and, in another twist, dignified annoyance at repeatedly being asked to say her name or to count from one to ten.

Most unexpected of all:

—I long for that young doctor.

She is referring to her neurosurgeon (strange that English uses possessive pronouns for such relationships), who is my age. She uses another of those untranslatable words, *akogareru*, expressing an admiring yearning that does not expect to be fulfilled. My grandmother has never betrayed an attraction to a male in the flesh, as opposed to the screen or the printed page. Was it such discipline that made it possible for her to live with my grandfather for over sixty years?

From My Grandmother's Bedside

Though her condition is too vast and abstract to talk about, she can refer to specific manifestations. One day she says to me, sadly,

—They're gone, aren't they.

—What's gone?

—My legs. I've been looking all over for them. But they're gone, aren't they.

I decide to sing to her. Melodies known to her from girlhood and young womanhood, familiar to me from childhood, from that vast, lovely repertory of art songs and songs written in the first decades of the century for schoolchildren (in many cases, as part of the official course of instruction) by Japanese composers thrilled by the encounter with lieder.

First Love (Hatsukoi)
Lying on my belly on the sand of a sand hill
day of recalling the faraway pain
    of first love

This is one of our shared favorites. The plainspoken lyricism of Ishikawa Takuboku, born the same year as my great-grandmother (1886), was gorgeously set to music by Koshigaya Tatsunosuke. I can't hit some of the high notes, but that doesn't matter. There's the familiar "Flowers" (Hana), composed by the talented Taki Rentarō, who was even able to study in Leipzig but contracted tuberculosis and died at the age of 24 in 1903; the deceptively innocuous "Red Dragonfly" (Aka tombo), which begins with a young child's memory of a red dragonfly seen at sunset over a nursemaid's shoulder, then moves on to how the nursemaid herself, married off at 15, no longer hears from home. The lyrics to "Red Dragonfly" are by the Symbolist poet Miki Rofū, and the song, composed by Yamada Kōsaku, one of Japan's outstanding modern composers, was released in 1922. Yamada's uninterrupted prominence through the war years now makes him vulnerable to the charge of war responsibility. Many of his achingly beautiful compositions are among our favorites. Cheerful songs are hard to find in this repertoire, but there's the bouncy "Stood Up" (Machibōke), also set to music by Yamada.

So far, so good. There's not much I can do about the lost sensation in her legs, but the singing seems to have distracted her. Flipping through the song book, I come upon "Pechika," for the Russian *pechka,* fireplace. It's another Yamada composition from 1925, the year before my grandmother had my mother, with lyrics by the poet Kitahara Hakushū. My pocket Japanese-English dictionary is inadvertently more helpful than larger dictionaries, for it offers as a translation of *pechka* "Manchurian stove." I knew the word couldn't be Japanese, but as with many sounds familiar from childhood I had never stopped to look it up. Is "Pechika" the relic of friendly intercourse between settlers and colonized, especially as remembered by the settlers?

The song is about the pleasures of a *pechka* on a snowy night. Outside it's cold, but inside it's "Burn, *pechka,* burn, let's tell stories, / from long, long ago." If there is such a thing as wistful coziness, this song captures it. I like it because I've associated it with my grandmother's growing up in the cold of Hokkaido.

But her brows furl in distress.

—Mother, come!

I've never heard her call her parents, though her father was alive until I was four or five. Her mother died in her late thirties, nursing her youngest, my granduncle, through a bout of dysentery.

—Mother, Father!

Turning to me imploringly,

—They won't come. I keep calling them, but they still won't come.

I call my mother, who is able to comfort her. Soon, my grandmother will begin calling her "Mother." And after the second stroke, she stops calling for anyone.

MISTAKE

—Would you like some of this, Obaachama?

I am eating green-tea-flavored ice with a dab of sweet adzuki bean paste. It's the kind of treat she and I favored.

She opens her eyes partway and looks at the plastic container I've thrust into her field of vision. Her bed is tilted up for her lunch feeding, and she looks uncomfortable. She wrinkles her nose and misery spreads over her face. I pull back the offending treat.

—I'm sorry, I'm sorry. I won't do anything you don't want.

Her features slowly relax. She's the last person in the world I'd want to make unhappy. That I came close to it revives her humanity for me.

SCALES

She weighs more than she did in health. The liquid diet is rich. The first summer, I was able to carry her to the bathroom every day and give her a shower. For two more summers, I was able to carry her in a rattan chair and set her near the television and the garden, but her diet was increased by 250cc of liquid food per day after the second stroke. Now, even I can barely turn her. My mother is smaller than I, smaller than her mother, and suffers from osteoporosis.

—Let's cut back her diet.

—We have to ask the doctor.

—We can tell the doctor we did it.

I have given up weighing my grandmother's life against my mother's in years, but I still do it in kilos.

Surprisingly, my mother doesn't put up a fight. Last year, when we had a similar problem, neither doctor thought it was necessary to cut back on her diet. Wasn't it a good thing she was able to gain weight? They are both tall men, and it is of course never their task to manipulate their patients' bodies. They reminded me of the quite lovely pediatrician in New York I encountered as a new mother who thought making my daughter's babyfood would help me feel more involved with her.

It was the Clinic Nurse who helped my mother decide it was all right to cut back on her mother's caloric intake.

My mother came of age when thinness was tubercular and plumpness a sign of wealth. (What remains valid today is the correlation of economic and bodily well being.) My mother herself contracted tuberculosis when I was of grammar-school age, and I was force-fed: two whole sandwiches a day in my lunchbox, both of which had to be eaten up because I went to school on a U.S. military base with fierce lunch monitors.

FRIEND UNKNOWN

She wasn't out this morning, but her wooden stool was. No cushion. It's cooler that way. No sign of the red-stringed kitty either.

The garden had already been watered. Garden? Among all the weeds were clumps of fragrant purple *shiso,* the "beefsteak plant." Looking at the dark traces on the soil, I could tell that the water had been splashed by hand from a pail. It helped me recognize a neglected site of democratic practice: even those who are quite well off here usually don't have much land, so what garden there is, whether a gardener-tended, pine-tree ringed lawn or a jerry-rigged plot spilling onto the street, is likely to be watered by hand from a pail, a watering can, or a hose, but certainly not from a sprinkler. So shrubs, pots, annuals, and even weeds receive human attention each morning.

Even more emboldened than before by my grandma's absence, I peer into the house, even run by it twice. There is a car squeezed against the side! Big bulletin boards on the street side of the house are covered with neighborhood announcements and a prominent notice that the house belongs to the neighborhood crime prevention network. So she, or more likely, her husband, must have been a personage of sorts.

A woman, middle-aged, emerges from some part of this pleasant disorder. Our eyes meet briefly—mine guilty, no doubt, and I hurry on. So she has a daughter-in-law. I wonder what she thinks of my grandma, that is, her mother-in-law. At least she lets her keep her distinctive costume. The front door, which is on the side but close enough to the street for me to take in without excessive indiscretion, is open, and there's a shelf filled with all kinds of items too small for me to identify. I like to imagine this is her collection of cherished miscellany.

MYSTERY

What is so appealing about her house is that it isn't apprehensible in a single glance. Most contemporary structures are. We know how to supply the sides of a box hidden from view without a second thought.

There used to be many such houses in the neighborhood. Several were on the way to the doctor's. I always went with my grandmother, and I loved anticipating and then passing the scary spots, which came closer and closer together as we approached the doctor's office. There was even a little playground with a fox shrine on top of a tumulus mound—perhaps the grave of an archaic notable. Two seesaws, a slide, and a few grandmothers with babies on their backs justified calling it a playground. Along with the bamboo groves of the house next door, the shrine disappeared; new playground equipment and a brightly painted bathroom were stuck in, along with an official sign detailing proper behavior for a public park. Another sign tells us that there were three tumulus mounds, not one, and that an archeological dig showed that each had been surrounded by a moat. The mound in the back, which I'd never noticed, had another sign designating the two young trees behind it as trees planted in honor of the marriage of the Crown Prince and Princess Masako.

The doctor's office was the old-fashioned kind. In winter we—mostly old folk, with whom he was immensely popular, plus my grandmother and me—huddled around a huge porcelain hibachi. In summer the front door was left open, and I could stare at the bamboo grove across the road that blocked part of the blazing blue sky and listen to the cicadas, almost succeeding in distracting myself from the dread of the injection no doubt in store for me.

It's just as well that electric heat and air-conditioning keep the door shut, now that this bamboo grove has been replaced by an anonymously cheerful structure.

The doctor's face was—thankfully, still is—round, and whatever the implement he fished out of his steaming autoclave, he almost never hurt me. The elderly, men and women, finished dressing in the waiting room. There was a social privacy that made this not only possible but natural.

But did this practice also make my curly brown hair invisible, so that my grandmother could sit calmly in that tiny room as if she'd brought a perfectly ordinary child? She had no choice: my mother stopped going out for several years after her bout of tuberculosis and the collapse of her marriage with the American. A school bus took me to and from school, but anywhere else I needed to go, it was my grandmother who had to deliver me. Our destinations were never pleasant—the dentist, the ear-nose-and-throat doctor, the eye doctor, or even the kindly internist who lived across from the bamboo grove; but my grandmother's deliberate pace and her delight in the features of each route, mostly people's gardens but also interesting houses or shops for which she had a special fondness, turned what might have been grim visits into enchanted outings.

Once, after her first stroke, when she was still able to take pleasure in my reading out loud to her from the essayists she had enjoyed more than a half-century earlier, it occurred to me to ask,

—You didn't mind taking a funny-looking kid to the doctor's?

She had been silent for some time, and I wasn't sure she heard. After a long pause, without turning or opening her eyes, she spoke.

—You weren't a funny-looking kid. You were a prize kid.

THE SAYABLE

I hadn't expected it. I hadn't expected anything. But I could never have asked her such a question when she was well. It was the intimacy that stroke gave us for a brief while.

That would have made for the sweetest parting.

But for all my fantasies, my grandmother has not lived and will not die for me.

Or for herself, I'm prompted to add, and then realize the absurdity of such statements.

After the first stroke, she spoke often, but she also moaned long and frequently. Does the replacement of the moans by warbles mean that she's in less pain? Today she gave one of her long, rambling, dismaying moans. Of course my mother rushed over. But there were words—the first in days—dissolved into the moan: because . . . it's [he's? she's?] adorable.

—Who's adorable, asked my mother delightedly. But it was too late. The answer vanished before our eyes, leaving what looked like the trace of a smile on her lips.

She isn't free of sad old habits, though. It's when she senses a crisis that she keeps her eyes wide open. She will not look at us, but her whole body bespeaks taut attention: an illustration of the homely phrase "to be all ears."

With no crisis in the air, she, and we, breathe and wait.

SCIENCE IN SOCIETY

When I gave birth to my son in Tokyo, I found myself living according to a communal rhythm for the five days I was in the hospital. At appointed times all the mothers went to the nursery together, weighed their babies, nursed them, weighed them again, and weighed the cast-off diapers, to register the hoped-for weight gains with each feeding. The feedings themselves were a time of remarkable tranquility. But the subsequent weighing was nerve-racking. If I had been a first-time mother, if I hadn't had an oversized baby that embarrassed the nurses—did he really belong to the species?—I would have felt an outright failure.

My mother learned to perform the same ritual for my grandmother in the hospital. Monitoring the amount of urine excreted each day was to guard against dehydration, promote the early detection of kidney problems, etc. No doubt. My mother has filled several notebooks with neatly ruled columns for temperature, blood pressure, and pulse rate as well as urine volume.

I've had a special aversion to the diaper-weighing. My grandmother was eighty-four at the time of her first stroke. There was no prospect of recovery. Such monitoring seemed burdensome in addition to everything else my mother had to do. For most of the first post-stroke year, she was exhorted to cook more varieties of tempting morsels for a nonexistent appetite: chewing is important, it's what keeps us human, you must find ways to get her to take some of her nourishment by mouth even though she has her feeding tube. So, other than breakfast, which was only fruit, yogurt, and perhaps cereal—varied in kind and flavor each day—my mother struggled to make five or six dishes each meal, in bite-sized portions, each bite chopped and mashed in the hopes of insertion into a fleetingly opened mouth. But more often than not, the jaws that allowed the baby spoon to deposit its load would simply clamp down after the metal was withdrawn and refuse to do their work. My mother's task was to coax and cajole, tap the rigid cheeks, then watch and wait for the sound and, especially reassuring, the sight of a swallow. When at last it came, it would be cheered. Sometimes, a breakfast bite would be hoarded inside one or the other cheek to be found at lunch. (My grandmother's fine teeth deteriorated. A nice dentist, again registered with the ward as being willing to make house calls, had to remove loosely attached shards of teeth so that she would not swallow them.)

Warnings about the weakened immune system of stroke patients, together with my grandmother's own legacy of germ anxiety, dictated that leftovers, though scrupulously refrigerated, could be offered only once, no later than one day after preparation. The smallest, most expensively packaged yogurts, custards, and jellies were bought to minimize waste from leftovers, since it was deemed that such packaged foods were likely to spoil even faster.

My mother never gained weight even during that period when, standing at the sink (not taking the time to sit at the table), she would scoop out the variously pale pink, green, orange, and cream-colored goop into her own mouth before tossing the plastic containers into the Noncombustible garbage container.

The lucky women here are the ones with a palpable break between the end of childcare (including and especially the supervision of studies until entrance into college) and the beginning of parent and/or in-law care. No doubt home care is the most desirable option for the elderly. And there are supports undreamed of in the United States, like the Clinic Nurse, barber and dentist visits, rental equipment, the national health insurance system underlying it all—for the moment. But the system relies disproportionately on women's resurrender to confinement. The home can be a lonely place; moreover, the care of the slow-dying elderly is too arduous to be imposed on solitary individuals, men or women. In Japan as elsewhere, discussion of the reorganization of work is motivated by interest in cost-cutting, thereby trading the possibility of a thoughtfully aging society for one of suppressed desperation.

The Clinic Nurse tells us there's a hospital in northern Japan where stroke patients, as soon as they are in stable condition, are taken into the bath with four or five nurses who manipulate their limbs. The benefits are dramatic. Why isn't such an approach generalizable? Because the insurance structure makes health-care delivery dependent on the dispensation of large volumes of pharmaceuticals rather than concentrated human labor.

In the meantime, my mother goes on weighing and recording. As with the frenetic cooking, she has been disciplined. That is, she has been made to believe in the importance of such a regimen, and her willing belief is the very substance of her discipline. Of course, it didn't begin with the onset of her mother's illness. It began at least with her schooling as a female subject of Imperial Japan and continued through interaction between that training, her personality, and the vicissitudes of her life.

What's so bad about it, I have to ask myself. Why do I resent it so much? It's given purpose to her days (now stretching into years) of caring for someone who will not get better. It taps into her schoolgirl strengths: quick at calculation, punctilious with note-taking. It helps to maintain her as a social being by reminding her of that competence. And she never, ever minds the repetition.

I resent it because I think that it perpetuates an illusion, the illusion that she can perpetuate her mother's life. But a less lofty voice inside me retorts, How do you expect her to get through every day, year after year?

But there must be more to my specific hatred of diaper-weighing. It's something to do with the grotesque deployment of scientific rationality for such an end. It's cynical, and my mother's earnestness is painful. Through exaggerated focus on simple bodily process, the use of scales—a simple instrument, but an instrument nonetheless—makes unbearably stark the reduction of my grandmother's being to the meanest biological function. And my mother's love to (unpaid) wage labor.

Bidden by no one, my mother kept an altogether different sort of record during her mother's first hospitalization. It was in a notebook tiny enough to be squeezed into a pocket so that it could be kept with her at all times. No neat columns, no figures march across its pages: instead, a hurried, almost scribbled transcription of the words uttered by my grandmother after she came out of her coma.

FRAGRANCE PRESERVED

And so I can't forgive my aunts' protecting themselves from the harshest tasks. My aunt next door performs this avoidance daily when she brings over fresh flowers. Or so it seems to me, because I can't accept that she genuinely believes in the curative power of flowers.

Once she brought over a single, perfectly formed bluish-pink rose on a bed of lace inside a glass dome. Smell, she said, lifting the dome. Sure enough, if you stuck your nose into the display, you caught a rose-scented whiff.

My grandmother never had artificial flowers of any kind in the house.

All right, so this is a real rose. After my aunt left, I lifted the dome for a closer look. There was a little packet under the petals dispensing the scent.

She left the dome on the cabinet in the entranceway. Visitors to the house of slow failing flesh will be greeted by this symbol of fragrance.

ENGINEERING

My other aunt's husband, retired from an impassioned career as a naval engineer, has sent pajamas he designed and sewed himself. He cut in half the traditional nightware, a gauze-lined summer kimono, and hemmed the top. The bottom half he turned into a rectangular loop, threaded elastic through the top (for the waist) and loose elastic through the bottom, sewing two pairs of snaps in the middle, which when unfastened left the garment skirtlike, and when closed remotely bloomerlike.

What prompted this innovation? My aunt was on the scene once when my grandmother was discharged from a hospital stay, and she was dismayed by how difficult it was to dress her mother modestly: kimonos always spread apart from the knees down, and her legs were too stiffly bent for tugging through ordinary pajama bottoms.

It wasn't a bad idea. But it's still hard for my mother to lift the lower half of her mother's body to get the deconstructible bloomers on. My aunt wouldn't know; it isn't labor she has shared in.

Garments for the bedridden who cannot participate in their own dressing have to open all the way down the front so that they can be rolled in. Weren't there analogous challenges on the ships my uncle designed? Or is this just another instance of the gap between theory and practice?

My aunt, for her part, says she is willing to take care of her mother if she can bring her to her own house in Nagasaki, far, far from Tokyo. She must know that's hardly feasible. Part of me is infuriated by her brazen suggestion, but another part is sadly glad to recognize it as the fantasy of having, at age 67, one's mother to oneself.

It finally occurs to me to wonder if the reason my mother never retorts, in response to her sisters' criticism that verges on abuse, Why don't you do it, then? is that she wouldn't want to give up her job.

RULERS

An assortment of rulers is part of the clutter of my big desk drawer in Chicago. The fetish began with a bamboo ruler belonging to my aunt in Nagasaki. Of course, when I took it I didn't know I was inaugurating a fetish; or, for that matter, that I would become estranged from its owner. I took it out of affectionate admiration for the name and class (grade 4, room 4) beautifully written with brush. The bamboo now shows a split on one end but without impairment to its functioning either as straight-edge or ruler: it still lies flat with sturdy integrity, and its markings are as clear as when purchased as a school supply for that fourth-grade year, nearly sixty years ago.

No wonder. Running a fingernail over its smooth surface, I see that the markings are fine, colored grooves. A precision instrument.

I have been driven to collect and half-conceal rulers in my desk because so many have disappeared into the erratic process of my son's homework. The plastic ones from Woolworth's or Walgreen's surface as purple, red, or blue shards. The wooden ones with a metal edge on one side are made of soft pressed fibers with markings stamped in light ink fated to fade before a single school year is over.

So I buy two new rulers in Japan, one for me, the other for my son. One is acrylic, the other vinyl. The features of each are enumerated on the packaging: on one the markings are internally laminated and permanently fadeproof, while the other has parallel translucent lines to facilitate "reading off" dictionary entries. They even come with warnings: don't bend, don't expose to high temperatures or paint thinner, don't poke one's own or other people's bodies and especially avoid the eyes.

My aunt's ruler is the length of a *shaku*, just a little short of a foot. It is graduated in *sun.* The acrylic and vinyl rulers are thirty centimeters long. I remember when Japan changed to the metric system. It seemed one of a host of postwar rehabilitative measures, like admission to the U.N. A commemorative stamp was issued, which my aunt bought for me. (She collected first-day-of-issue covers for me.)

When I struggled to memorize pints, gallons, quarts, rods, bushels, inches, miles, and feet, I was unconvinced of the superiority of the metric system. Now my son's rulers, the fragments and about-to-become fragments, are marked in both centimeters and inches. They are unfussy and undemanding. The Japanese rulers anticipate diligent students burning midnight oil as they mark columns in their notebooks and copy out definitions.

My aunt's ruler must have passed into general household use. Its smudges are the traces of countless tasks performed by her, my grandfather, my grandmother, and my mother. For that, and for the beautiful calligraphy of the talented child who became my aunt, it has a special place in my clutter.

IT ISN'T ABOUT MONEY

By the time he died, ten months after his wife's first stroke, my grandfather was ninety-four years old, and he had been married to my grandmother for sixty-seven years. No wonder he declined so quickly after her hospitalization: he must not have been able to imagine being cared for by anyone else.

(And who else would have cured a sudden onset of senility with a diet of detective fiction, and just as quickly withdrawn it when the diet proved so successful that addiction and red eyes set in?)

The inheritance their daughters are fighting over centers on the rental rights to the land my grandparents have lived on since the war. Real estate in Japan has dizzied plenty of people over the last two or three decades. But I assume that the struggle is also a translation, for which the law provides only a crude syntax, of wants unmet in time, wants the sisters themselves probably can't identify.

BUT IT IS

Leaving a reception where there had been heated exchange over the propriety of cooperating with the government plan to set up a private fund (in lieu of government compensation) to benefit women in Asia, notably the women and girls who had been rounded up as sex slaves for the Japanese Imperial Army and known as comfort women, I overheard one man say to another, It isn't about money.

I wonder what you know about lost dignity, I felt like saying to the man. Or if you've ever truly wanted for money.

Of course, Japan must extend a sincere apology, including and especially public rectification of the historical record in textbooks. But the recipient of an apology can't clothe herself in words. Nor will properly collected money cheer her in the grave. Only money now can secure the semblance of a regular history, and therefore of dignity in the ways of the world.

DIVINE WIND: THE SPECIAL ATTACK CORPS

Why are they all so handsome, the young men—boys, many of them—at least in the photos? And their letters so beautifully written, with brush, often explicitly cast as last testaments to their families. Always an apology for not being able to return the kindness of their parents, for going ahead of them . . .

They're equipped with goggles, fur-lined hats with ear flaps, and those long silk scarves. No wonder they look glamorous: the aviator, soaring hero of modernity.

But the Tokkō ("kamikaze") pilots were more accurately parts of machines, machines that were replacements for beasts of burden insofar as they were nothing more than bearers of bombs. (Nonpilots were liable to be made naked beasts of burden, like those who had to run into American tanks with bombs strapped to their backs. Intermediate between the Tokkō pilots and the human torpedoes in their metal coffins on the one hand and the backpack bomb carriers on the other were men in special wet suits allegedly designed to recycle human exhalation, thus enabling them to stand underwater for hours on end, waiting for American vessels to pass over their bamboo poles with bombs attached to the tips.)

The pilot's fashionable garb mocks the parental devotion expended in rearing sons fated to be offered up to such use. No wonder one mother said, when unconditional surrender was announced, We will have to have him die. "Him" was Vice Admiral Ōnishi Ryūtarō, the author of the kamikaze operation. Ōnishi committed suicide.

Some mothers committed suicide themselves. One hanged herself in the shed after seeing her son and learning that he had been assigned on a one-way mission. She did not want to be a distraction in his thoughts when the time came for him to do his duty. Since the remains of kamikaze pilots could hardly be returned to their families, it was common practice to send ahead locks of hair and nail clippings. One son who had done so ended up not having to fly his mission. When he came home, he learned that his mother had drowned herself upon receipt of his package.

These days, the television screens are filled with these beautiful photos and letters as well as greying men and women who say, incredulously, How could we have believed what we were told? And having no answer, they embark on campaigns to tell their stories. Surely no one will be so foolishly credulous again?

A Tokkō pilot talks with young students at his university. They say, reading the letters and wills of the drafted students, they can understand that their motives were pure, that they were willing to sacrifice themselves for their country.

The balding pilot says, We weren't so pure. We were all subject to "mind control."

He is referring to the great contribution that the Aum sect made to the anniversary year. The phrase "mind control" has given many, many Japanese a tool with which to think about citizenship in the prewar and wartime nation state. Along with espousing an ersatz ensemble of eastern religious beliefs and practices, Aum members manufactured Sarin and other deadly gases, and used sci-fi tactics against critics as well as members who turned skeptical. The sect's bizarre and horrifying experiments resonate with the germ warfare and vivisection research conducted by Unit 731, the most notorious of the Japanese military's "medical" experimentation units in China; but it is the sect's astonishing success in indoctrination that has put the phrase "mind control" on everyone's lips and prompted a conceptual leap in understanding the wartime past.

As for the present: why young Japanese, many of them academically successful and destined for bright futures, turned to Aum is a pressing question for this still remarkably prosperous society. Meanwhile, the media will fatten and feed off the wretched Aum stars as long as, and only as long as, they sell.

MOURNING, FOR THE FUTURE?

People are busy writing. They are collecting and publishing the writings of their beloved dead; they are struggling to remember their lives during and after the war, before the economic miracle; they are writing new children's stories and translating them into French and English.

There is a frenzy of writing.

There is also speaking and traveling. Teachers visit the relatives of students whom they fear having sent to their deaths. A man travels to southern China to the site where his company, Unit 8406, hitherto undiscussed, was engaged in germ warfare. He finds a younger man, now middle-aged, who was one of the subjects deliberately infected with malaria. He bows and asks his forgiveness. The younger man smiles, tells him not to worry. He was young when it happened, he does not remember clearly, he can forgive the old man. The old man is driven by the need to speak, for no one else from his unit has disclosed its history.

Most heartbreaking is the story of another old man who never told his wife that he had belonged to Unit 731. He had witnessed and participated in what would literally become unspeakable horror. He never took a regular job, rejected all opportunities for promotion, and avoided friendship. If the Americans ever found out what he'd been involved in, his superiors had told him at the time of the unit's frantic disbanding, they'd execute him for sure. (The United States, interested in the research of Unit 731, refused to have it aired during the Tokyo Trial.) A traveling exhibit on Unit 731 came to the man's region for the fiftieth anniversary. He made up his mind to go. And seeing the exhibit, he decided to release his fifty-year-old secret.

Many couples were separated at the end of the war in Manchuria, the husband sent off to labor camps in Siberia and the wife perhaps killing their children before the onslaught of Soviet troops. A friend tells me it is not uncommon for such couples to neither ask nor tell one another what happened to the children.

August 1995 also marks the tenth anniversary of the terrible mountainside crash of a packed Japan Airlines 747 flight headed for Osaka. Over the years, the bereaved have cleared a path up the mountain and erected a memorial. Watching them wave lights at the night sky at the hour of the crash, hearing a father shouting his son's name (he can only do it once a year, he says, because back home he has to worry about the neighbors), I can't help feeling that I've arrogantly underestimated the degree to which people continue to feel linked to their dead.

It is said that people in the area who happened to have heard the crash, who couldn't rid their minds of the sound but felt awkward about visiting the memorial, found themselves both able and driven to join this year.

Many families think of their memorializing as a way to press for air traffic safety so that other families will not have to experience their grief.

Japan Air Lines, which has supported the memorializing, intends to put paid to its involvement with this anniversary.

AUGUST 15, 1995 (I)

The Anniversary of a Lie . . .

All right. So he's going to have to stand in the great hall with the man's son in an hour.

Still.

Murayama Tomiichi, the Socialist who became prime minister for the Liberal Democrats, the enemy that gave his own party, insofar as it stood for pacifism, its identity throughout the postwar years, held a press conference just an hour before the state memorial service for the war dead and referred to "errors" in "state policy" that had led to invasion and colonization.

If you're willing to be that explicit about mistaken state policy, are you including the emperor, asked a reporter.

No, no, said the genial and decent Mr. Murayama. That the emperor had no responsibility was established at the end of the war both in our country and abroad. We know His Majesty aspired tirelessly for peace and made the final decision to end that war.

Is it because Murayama thinks a bullet-proof vest would be unbearably hot? Or that a bullet-proof helmet wouldn't go with the trademark eyebrows? Or is it that power has become too sweet, even or especially for an old-time Japanese socialist?

I should bite my tongue.

No one should demand of another that he put his life at risk.

But the office of prime minister brings with it obligations exceeding those demanded of ordinary citizens. And those special obligations are assumed by choice.

But even a prime minister can't be required to be a hero.

The prime minister's life can be better protected than the lives of ordinary citizens.

But democracy shouldn't depend on heroes.

Democracy does require citizens who take politics seriously.

That's hard to sustain, anywhere in the world. And heroes are undeniably precious. Even necessary. In Japan the last person who publicly referred to the emperor's partial (that is, shared) responsibility for the war got a bullet in his lungs. That was then-Mayor Motoshima of the city of Nagasaki, who spoke out in 1989 as the emperor lay dying.

It's not as if the emperor were so important today, or people especially interested in him. They aren't. Nor even that the emperor's role in the war is the most urgent topic for rethinking. It's that the fiction of the emperor's *utter* nonresponsibility has worked like an invisible thread through the tissue of postwar Japan, forming nodes with other threads, making them invisible, too. This system of invisibility is also a system of unspeakability. If you can't talk about something you know you see, you may stop seeing it. If you stop talking, others, particularly people born after you, may never know there was anything to be seen.

What if the prime minister had been willing to say on this day, in that setting, Yes, the late emperor, together with others, was responsible for Japan's role in the last world war, and yes, it is truly unfortunate that he could not have publicly acknowledged it for the sake of the Japanese people and the world.

The content is banal; yet had the Prime Minister uttered those words, time would have stopped in Japan. Once the unsayable is said, especially by a person of authority, it might become sayable by others. And that would give the flesh and blood of social actuality to the ghostly figments of bitter or confused memory banished as useless from most minds. And a wave of seeing and hearing might have washed over the nation: the advent of political seriousness.

Maybe.

Instead, Mr. Murayama recited from a prepared response. We know he had aspired for a genuine apology resolution by the Parliament. That failed. Then he had wanted an international gathering for the fiftieth anniversary to be held on the fifteenth. But no, the LDP party bosses didn't think the time was ripe. So he ended up staking everything on a brief press conference preceding the state ritual. Picking out the strongest words from the tired vocabulary of national apology, he strung them together in an eye-catching but safe combination.

Everybody knew he hadn't wanted to continue as prime minister after his own party's massive defeat in the Upper House elections. But it was inconvenient for the LDP to have the coalition fall apart. So there he was, stretching still further the veneer of legitimacy over a politics that will necessarily remain a frivolous and obscure game played by professional politicians, mostly men, trading on personal and factional interest.

How can any notion of responsibility operate here? Everybody knows that the system of taboos emanating from the emperor and the interpretation of the war is literally maintained by the threat of violence embodied in a small group of rightists. But why should an entire society, and so many apparently unrelated aspects of social life, be governed in this way?

Taboos are alibi machines. People understand if you don't want to challenge a taboo, and by extending you their understanding they also keep themselves off the hook. Most Japanese wouldn't dream of reproaching Murayama for denying imperial responsibility. The United States was in at the beginning on not bringing the emperor to trial, but Japanese citizens and leaders together have turned the emperor's nonresponsibility into the founding myth of postwar Japan. Respecting a taboo enforced by a few has gone hand-in-hand with acquiescence to a politics that collaborates in the maintenance of a coercive school and work life for most citizens.

Remembering Mr. Murayama's well-oiled performance, I find myself wishing for a stammer, even a pause: some sign of recognition that he was perpetuating a national lie on a day when it counted.

. . . And the Treacherous Terrain of Peace

If structures aren't changed by individuals, what are the obligations of leaders? Can leaders exist at all today? How will Nelson Mandela or Aung San Suu Kyi—if she and her movement are ever successful—manage in the long, long days after the glory of liberation? That surely depends on the quality of democracy able to develop around them. And what will be more threatening—a past too corrosive to be faced, the tenacity of barbaric inequities, the bewitching rewards of multinational corporations? Or the way everyday life keeps you going and keeps you drained at the same time?

From My Grandmother's Bedside

AUGUST 15, 1995 (II)

In Seoul, the finial was removed from the dome of the Japanese colonial capitol.

In front of the Brandenburg Gate in Berlin, a group of Japanese peace activists opened nine bottles of wine put away at the Yalta Conference for fifty years later, when, as FDR wrote, the whole world would be at peace. The group shared the wine with German passersby.

They could equally have brought the wine to Seoul. Maybe aesthetically, gustatorially, it wasn't an appealing choice, given the deadly heat of the East Asian summer. But there is the fact that VE Day was three months ago, in May. Once again, the slogan for Japanese modernity rears its head: exit Asia, enter Europe.

THE LIGHTNESS AND HEAVINESS OF WORDS

Leaders abroad are reacting favorably to Mr. Murayama's statement. But they aren't thinking of the military comfort women, or the forced laborers kept alive for as long as they happened to last on rotting potatoes, or the families of colonized subjects executed as Class B and C war criminals, to whom the Japanese government has resolutely refused individual compensation. Mr. Murayama reiterated that all such matters had been resolved between governments.

They scattered, said Prime Minister Murayama of the war dead. "Scattered" is as in cherry blossoms scattering. A dangerous metaphor for shattered bone, torn ligament, spilled blood.

Please, Mr. Prime Minister, how about a little verbal hygiene? Of course, he's a busy politician. He doesn't live on an academic calendar—he doesn't have time to meditate on Language. So he uses the standard expressions of his generation.

And perhaps undue weight shouldn't be attached, pedantically, to such practices. But words are being made to count for a lot—for everything, in fact, insofar as all governmental compensation has been refused. How can the words "We are sorry"—any words, for that matter, standing alone, unadorned (where not contradicted) by action—offer proof of their utterer's sincerity?

On the other hand, when President Clinton affirmed his support of Truman's decision to use the atomic bombs back in April, many Japanese were horrified, and his American male geniality suddenly began to look like superficiality or stupidity.

—I've decided I hate Clinton, my mother said one spring day, by international telephone.

—Why now, I wondered mildly.

—Because he said Truman was right.

If I place myself on one side of the International Date Line, I share in that reaction; on the other, I can only summon cynicism toward words uttered out of political convenience, more and more wearing the aspect of necessity as the presidential election approaches.

LANGUAGE LESSON

Reading the section in Gar Alperovitz's new book on the bomb about how information was kept from the American public, I'm stopped by the term *classification.* That, says Alperovitz, was the most common, the routine way in which information was kept from the citizenry.

It makes perfect sense. That's how bureaucracies work. That's not what caught me up short. It's the evolution of word usage, whereby a word designating a seemingly neutral process—categorization—is narrowed and specialized so that it refers to categorization that produces secrets. Then again, history has numerous examples that show how a process like categorization is never neutral. Language use, in extending meaning, and bureaucracies, in maintaining routine, can preserve the semblance of neutrality, or even innocence. Alperovitz puts *classification* in quotation marks, suggesting that it's a euphemism.

I can't remember learning that use of the word, looking it up in the dictionary when the more general meaning wouldn't fit the context. I must have intuited it and hoarded it as part of my special knowledge of Americans, like the syllables to utter at passport renewal time, the mores of slumber parties, the names for body parts not always in the dictionary, or religious customs, most of my friends being missionaries' daughters.

During one of my first two or three days in the American world—that is, in the school for U.S. military dependents stationed abroad—I was repeatedly dragged into the playground at recess by another child who insisted, "You're not s'posed to," looking at the classroom. Studying such words and practices exhausted my resources and left no room for irony. I was ferreting out American secrets in order to inch closer to full citizenship.

BIRTHDAY PARTY

My mother baked a cake for my birthday every year, and invited the three sons of my granduncle across the street and my friend next door, but I myself went to only two birthday parties. The first was for a boy I hardly knew. He was the son of my family's dressmaker and a business acquaintance of my grandfather. His mother used a fancy French name. His father was half English, which left him three-fourths Japanese. I was slightly taller, and maybe spoke more English, which didn't say much for him. But somehow I understood that he was rich: his house was big, and it came with a terrace and a grassy garden uncluttered with plants (I wouldn't have the name or concept of *lawn* for a few more years). And he had big girls over, all of whom knew each other, so I hung back.

The second birthday party was for a classmate at the kindergarten I attended on a U.S. Army base. My mother had a wine-red velvet dress with navy blue trim on the sleeves made for me, though not by the dressmaker with the French name, for that would have been too expensive. She and my father took me to Mitsukoshi Department Store, which must have been just recovering its grandeur, with an organist at the pipe organ, sending notes shuddering over every floor. My mother chose a purse for the birthday child.

Delivered to the party site (the officers' club on the base?) I had no idea which girl was celebrating her birthday. My dress was unlike any of the others. Theirs were gauzy, probably of cotton organdy or perhaps, already, nylon, in pastel shades with lots of ruffles and lace. I think it was my father who picked out the host, whereupon I set off in pursuit across a vast floor. When I finally caught up, I tapped her on the shoulder (I still didn't know her name) under a blond pigtail. She turned around briefly, took the box silently thrust at her, and continued to walk away.

That is the last time I remember going out with both parents. I wouldn't have the chance to party again until junior high school. That was with a small group of mostly, and no doubt justly, unpopular girls. (We wrote our notes to each other in Latin.) The form of celebration still puzzled me— steak with waffles for breakfast—but at least I had found a group to do something apparently normal with.

STRATEGY

Speaking by telephone for the first time in fifteen years, my old friend, the girl next door, tells me how vividly she remembers the chagrin she felt upon discovering, when we were about ten, that I knew Chinese characters she didn't. I have no memory of this. I tell her it's impossible, that at most I could have known only the numbers, my address, and maybe simple characters like those for *eye, moon, sun, hand.* She claims I would write down characters I knew to see if she could read them.

So this is how I survived my American Schooling? And this accomplished teacher of young children is not only willing but wishing to revive the friendship?

She also tells me that I had beautiful clothes, dream clothes in the eyes of someone like her, the youngest of four in a postwar family. When pictures were taken of the two of us, she rued the knees that were so conspicuous under her short skirts. She heard me practice the violin and envied me.

I have to remind her that I only got as far as "Twinkle, Twinkle, Little Star." It was one of the shorter-lived of my mother's very sporadic efforts at my bourgeoisification. After the third or fourth lesson, I let my tired arm drop the rental violin, and that was the end of that.

THE EXPRESSIVITY OF EXTREMITIES

My mother belongs to that generation whose coming of age coincided with the War. A generation of young men and women lost the chance to fret about their looks, model their clothing and gestures after Hollywood cinema, or simply to sit with their books. "When I was my most beautiful / Town after town came tumbling down / And blue sky would show up in shocking places," writes the distinguished poet Ibaragi Noriko, born the same year as my mother. "Lots of people around me died / And I lost my chance for dressing up."

Nevertheless, early postwar pictures of my mother show a pretty young woman with verve, the effect of shoulder-length permed hair and, especially, fitted American coats and suits with flared skirts. And her baby—me—is remarkably fat, thanks to my mother and grandmother's antitubercular passion supported by my father's U.S. military purchasing power. After toddlerhood, through my middle childhood, there are almost no pictures of my mother. She in fact contracted tuberculosis, and her marriage ended. When she finally reappears, in photos from my young adulthood, she has short, straight hair, and a clear-eyed, girlish look. I never gave much thought to my family's preternatural youthfulness, chalking it off to tribal peculiarity and even in a general way to ethnicity, so often had I heard it said that you never can tell a foreigner's age, meaning always a white person, and really an American. But now I am puzzled by how such troubled lives could yield these female countenances. In my mother's case, I wonder if the eight-year marriage to an American GI was so improbable that, in spite of its indignities, it had literally failed to leave much of an impression. It marked her life, but its direct impact was brief, and she never had to accommodate the slower oppression of an ordinary marriage.

I have been startled by glimpses of her sleeping hands. They are all bone and knuckle, a thin dry sheet of skin barely containing the assortment of ill-aligned protrusions. Even in summer her skin bears the traces of winter cracks. The bent, disfigured nails are hidden during the cold months by bandages in various stages of slippage.

My grandmother's hands were never like these. They were huge working hands, a startling interruption of her elegance. But having grown up with her, I want to say it is unimaginative to deem the signs of physical labor antithetical to elegance. My grandmother's hands were sturdy and reliable, good at trimming bushes, mending tears in delicate fabrics, ironing ruffled dresses as well as my grandfather's shirts on a cushion on the floor. Her blunt fingertips could count through stacks of postcard-sized photographs—the goods of my grandfather's business—faster than anyone else. In one swoop they fanned out a stack as if it were no more than a deck of cards and marked off unerring fives, her mind holding onto the sum through constant disruption from family and world. Her feet held her erect through hours at the paper cutter trimming those photos, or at the stove preparing a remarkable array of dishes with little planning or reference to cookbooks.

Within two months of her first stroke, her hands became soft and smooth, and the fingertips began to taper. Was this their original form during her privileged girlhood?

My mother has made a ritual of rubbing aloe into her mother's hands and feet. The nurses can never get over how soft they are, she beams.

Even the knobby callus on the side of the foot above each heel that fascinated me—as if it were an optional appendage unbestowed upon me—has disappeared. Now I know the knob is common on the feet of women and even of men who had to sit formally on the floor, their legs folded compactly under them. My grandmother can no longer sit at all. Stroke has given her maidenly hands and feet.

Even in summer, the soles of my mother's feet are mapped out with bandaids, tracing a futile battle against peeling skin. They have extravagant bunions, like her father's and like mine. Add to this their childlike size and it becomes a challenge to keep them shod. Just to make it a little harder, this year the second toe on her right foot has begun to ride on the big toe.

NIGHT SOUNDS

On one of my first nights home, wakeful with jet lag, I heard a rapid succession of shuffles downstairs. It was my mother getting up to go to the bathroom. She never moves slowly, however short the distance or unpressing her purpose. I have mocked and scolded her haste, since she is given to stumbling and stubbing herself. (But I suspect my harshness is motivated by the ungainliness I share with her.)

That night I heard her footsteps as the noise she will make on winter nights when I am no longer there, when no one is there to hear it.

Now, I watch as she dozes off in the deep heat of midafternoon. My grandmother emits a sound, and my mother, instantly shaking off sleep, propels herself to her bedside. I notice, for the first time, that she has developed the gait of an old woman.

TRADING CONFESSIONS

Late in my stay, my aunt next door launches one of her unpredictable attacks, of the sort that has devastated my mother and grandmother over the years. Unlike the weather, their only harbinger is the stomach-knotting instinct in her habitual targets that they are due for a storm.

My uncle joins in this one. The presence of male authority unmitigated by blood tie doubles our humiliation. My jaws stiff in misery, I say to my mother,

—I don't know how you've managed all this time. I think you're tougher than I am.

To which she replies with genuine sympathy,

—I'm just insensitive.

APOLOGY AND FORGIVENESS

A friend, a philosopher by trade and by conviction, supposes that we forgive others so as not to be debilitated by the past. I, too, had been thinking that in the end we apologize for our own sake. I had been brooding about national apologies for historic wrongs and the common retort: "I wasn't even born then."

Wouldn't it be funny, my friend continues, if nothing really gets exchanged after terrible wrongs are committed?

An apology is offered, forgiveness is granted. We do it for ourselves so that we can go on living with others.

It wouldn't happen in my family. Maybe this is so in most families. Intimacy raises the hurdle of beginnings, because too much mutual knowledge makes it seem unlikely that the future will be different from the past.

ANNIVERSARIES FOR UNREMEMBERING

In my house in Chicago, I can't turn to a bookcase or open a drawer without coming across a gift from my aunts and uncles. I was the first, and as it turned out only, female grandchild, the first niece, an only child several times over in the family for many years. My grandmother, my two unmarried aunts, and later their husbands enveloped me with stories, outings, stamps, games, and, always, anxious watching, their attention seeming to make the odd child more precious for her oddity. Now my house holds vases in lacquered wood or porcelain, tie-died silk scarves, paintings, tablecloths, books, dolls and wooden toys for my children, ties for my husband. Some are beautiful objects that suit my taste; others do not. And some are ordinary but chosen with care. Should I think of them as grown cold now that the love with which they were given has been withdrawn?

I can't.

I can't think of the past as canceled by the present, from good to bad any more than from bad to good. The affection once lavished on me and mine is locked away in those objects.

Every few years, I reluctantly use chlorine bleach to clean the blackening bottom of my favorite wooden cutting board, just as my aunt in Nagasaki does with hers though with greater frequency. I can't cancel out habits of speech and gesture and tastes absorbed from them, even the ones formed in reaction to theirs.

In the meantime, I have to draw lines through dates, mostly birthdays, still imprinted on my memory. Don't worry about Christmas presents for them any more. They will not be welcome from me, their sister's daughter. Thus tattered is my grandmother's nest.

Learning to unnotice the anniversary dates of the adults who scolded and protected me brings back a poem by W. S. Merwin about how we pass the anniversary-to-be of our own deaths: "Every year without knowing it I have passed the day / When the last fires will wave to me / And the silence will set out. . . ."

I MISSED YOU FROM THE BEGINNING

I've dreaded my grandmother's death for almost as long as I can remember. Ever since I isolated the knowledge of death as fear of death. She was the first person to whom I confessed my fear of dying. She must have been in her early forties then. We were in the bath together. She laughed and said, Look how old I am. I'm not afraid of dying.

And still my fear of death consolidated as fear of her death. Not long after we got our first TV set (cast off by my father when he permanently left Japan—an American television, an Emerson I think, in Japan!), my mother, grandmother, and I watched Robert Bresson's *Diary of a Country Priest* (*Le Journal d'un curé de campagne*) together. We were all three spellbound by the slow, still depiction of the journey of a soul against the black-and-white of that French countryside. It was the beginning of my summer vacation. Thereafter the Tokyo sunlight could only seem harsh, for the darkness on the screen had become a prefiguration of my grandmother's death.

Bresson's film was made in 1950. We saw it on the government channel in 1958. The previous summer, when I was turning ten, my grandmother and I were apart for the first time. She was hospitalized for forty days for a hysterectomy. Of course I wasn't told what it was. She came home thin, her elegance accentuated by a black suit. Her eyes—a lighter brown than any in the family, for which we teased her, saying she had Caucasian blood, probably White Russian—had an improbable sparkle as she greeted me. Only then did I realize how lonely I had been in the shadowy house without the steady movement of her white apron to follow through the day.

I couldn't know then that I was to have many, many more summers with her, summers that I would spend profligately.

SUMMER MANLINESS

The sun has set, but the heat shows no signs of abating in the street filled with evening shoppers—mothers hustling their toddlers as they pick up dinner fixings and chat with neighbors and shopkeepers; suited men and young women pouring out of the station, steps brisk and eyes resolute in spite of the bicycles (some baskets filled with a miniature dog or two instead of vegetables); strollers; grandmas with canes and walkers. At this hour, in such places, Japan becomes Old Worldly.

Drugged with the heat and content to be swept along by the crowd, I halted before the spectacle of three young men coming from the opposite direction. Judging from the shape of their bundles, they must have come from the public bath. They might have been construction workers, dressed in white t-shirts and the traditional laborer's garb of knickerbocker-like trousers ending in the dark, rubber-soled slippers that offer secure footing on telephone poles, scaffolding, or manholes. (When these pants suddenly began to appear in cobalt blue and burnt orange instead of dark navy, I asked an elderly gardener what they were called. They were jockey pants, he told me.) The three had twisted towels tied headband style around their foreheads. Walking three abreast—something no one else did on that narrow street—and brimming with vitality from the bath, they overwhelmed the torpor of the dusty crowd.

SUMMER WIND

Sometimes, in a valley of condominiums under construction, a wind will rise from nowhere. I say from nowhere because I can't see it. All the trees have been cut down to make room for the handsome boxes where new dreams will be dreamt. This is the neighborhood where my grandmother took me with my friend next door to buy a star festival bamboo many Julys ago.

I can't decide whether I'm a ghost or a fetus as I lift my arms to catch more of the wind.

METROPOLITAN DOG LIFE

A year or so ago, used plastic water bottles, plastic barley-tea bottles, two-liter plastic anything bottles began to appear on the street, capped, filled with water, and placed with obvious design at intervals along walls and tied around telephone poles. No one could tell me what they were for. I learned that the bottles were called "pet bottles." This turned out to be a nonclue, or rather a misleading clue, as I realized when "pet," or rather *petto,* turned out to be "PET"—polyethylene terepthalate. Finally, I heard that these were anti-dog-marking devices. The theory was that the blinding flash emitted by water-filled plastic bottles refracting sunlight would—distract dogs from the urge? make them do it in front of someone else's house? cause kidney infection, resulting in the eventual disappearance of dogs from Tokyo?

My mother tells me she read that the bottles were found not to work. But they have not disappeared.

BREAD AND CLASS

The Clinic Nurse brought over half a delicious apple pie to share with my mother, the Home Helper, and me. It was from a neighborhood bakery that I had managed not to notice.

It turned out to occupy part of the old "market" lot, around the corner from the bath house. It is a cunning structure with burnt red tile meant to look like brick. A mini-minitruck delivers the bread from the factory every morning. The whole enterprise is rescued from terminal cuteness by the occasional presence of a baby carriage with a real baby needing to be rocked, and by the bread that is sold.

I'm an aficionado of *anpan*, rolls filled with sweet adzuki-bean paste. My grandmother and I like the kind filled with coarsely mashed beans; my mother prefers the pureed kind, in which, to our mind, the beanness of the bean has been defeated. This store has not only the pureed and mashed paste rolls (distinguishable by the exquisitely contrastive salt-preserved cherry blossom in the "navel" of the pureed roll) and the increasingly common French-bread *anpan* but also the increasingly rare "nightingale" roll, filled with green bean paste. (The Japanese nightingale gives its name to a shade of green.)

I know it's not a taste shared by many nowadays, I say consolingly to the mistress apologetic for being sold out. Ah, but it has its following, she says, as if to rescue me from peculiarity. We never have any left at the end of the day. They're delivered at ten in the morning. If you come before noon, we'll be sure to have some.

What attests to the store's seriousness is its two grades of unsliced white bread, standard and superior. The price difference is about fifty cents (at the ephemeral rate of one hundred yen to the dollar). There are old-fashioned names for these grades, *nami* and *jō*. These are terms that can be applied to bowls of noodles or rice (with tempura or pork cutlets on top, say), fixed lunches, or sushi. What's nice about these categories, I realize, is that in principle nothing is wrong with *nami*.

Nami usually doesn't come with fancy extras. If it's sushi, the superior grade might include (in addition to the standard fare of shrimp, squid, tuna, and egg) oily tuna, roe, or sea urchin, none of which my family likes. Honoring the spirit of ordinariness, I resist the temptation to buy "superior" bread and get the "standard," which turns out to make superb toast, crisp on the outside, moist but not chewy on the inside.

Another system of food classification is pine-bamboo-plum, or *shōchikubai*, three felicitous plants that preserve their green or blossom in winter. You're not embarrassed to order the pine meal, though it might be visibly more modest than the plum.

Even if it's just a matter of name, it's different from first, second, and third class, as on the trains my aunt traveled in when she married the naval engineer and left Tokyo. Then she sat for well over twenty-four hours on straight-backed seats, three to a seat, facing three others, decorum preventing her from stretching her feet the tiniest bit.

MORNING

When my daughter was two, I brought her from Brooklyn for a summer with her grandmothers in Tokyo. She would be starting nursery school in the fall. I brought an album of pictures of the neighborhood, thinking they would help her hang on to a reality that might otherwise sink into the other side of the ocean. I was assuming she would suffer the same dislocation of eyes, ears, and tongue (for food and for speech) following transpacific crossings that I did.

One morning, a month or more into our stay, when she was between sets of sound, taste, and smell, her father came to join us. He arrived at night after she was asleep. As the sun streamed in through the eastern windows of her room, she began her morning murmurs, and we went in. She looked out from the bars of her crib. Then, as I remember it, her body was transfixed in a quiver.

The memory of that sensation was stirred again at my grandmother's bedside. I came up to her as I had many other mornings, only this time she looked up at me and sighed. Then a shudder of recognition traveled through her body. A light came into her eyes and turned into a beam powerful enough to swallow my face. Then it faded.

Twenty years ago my daughter was on the anticipatory side of language; today, my grandmother is beyond language. I've learned from each how the body expresses recognition as love.

In a song called "Mother," from the suite *The Morning of the Beautiful Farewell,* a woman on her deathbed recalls her own dead mother of thirty years ago. She asks, with embarrassment, for the kimono that the mother, younger then than she is now, had carefully folded and put away for her; confesses that she wants to smell the smell of her mother; asks, finally, to be dressed in the kimono. In a crescendo she cries out to her mother, demands that she not leave her, that she get rid of the night.

At the end of each day, my mother goes to her mother's bedside with a baby toothbrush dipped in liquid toothpaste. She drapes the plastic apron over her and announces the last brushing of the day, repeating the date portion of her morning greeting. Ever so tenderly, she seeks an opening to insert the brush and cleanse the interior of that uneating, uncomplaining mouth. She wipes the lips, removes the apron, bids her good night, and turns off the overhead light.

But my grandmother is not left in utter darkness. To one side, the small alcove light burns through the night. On the other, my mother sleeps her tired sleep, ready to stumble to an unformed sound.

EPILOGUE TOWARD AN UNKNOWN ENDING

Often, before running the dog on a Chicago winter morning, I will reach into the freezer for a sugared kumquat. The intense sweetness coupled with bitterness is fortifying for the expedition, I say to myself.

It was a cold March that followed my grandmother's stroke. A nondescript fruit store stood at the bottom of the steep hill leading to her hospital. Maybe it was the stinging wind that made me pause before the mountain of plastic bags filled with the new crop of kumquats, their coating of sugar like snow on bright orange jewels. Without hesitation I reached into my purse and walked out with one heavy bag.

Kumquat steeped in boiling water: good for colds, soothing to the throat. It should be sipped, letting the fragrant steam curl into the nostrils as the sugar eddies into the water, leaving the skin of the fruit translucent and more jewel-like than ever in the bottom of the cup. It's the sort of remedy my grandmother might have proposed, though she didn't. She planted a kumquat bush in the garden after I was grown and gone. Its branches were heavy with fruit in the winter, and the years when she had the time—when business was bad—she would candy the ones that would otherwise have gone uneaten and spoiled.

Now there's only one sugared kumquat left in the bag from the store at the foot of the hill. I've stopped reaching into the freezer.

· · ·

Someone on the radio is talking about growing vegetables in the winter in Maine. You use a cold frame, a bottomless box with a glass top. *Fu-re-e-mu.* The syllables come back to me from radio and, later, TV shows on gardening aired at odd hours, usually early in the morning. My grandmother listened to them avidly; if a program started and she was working outside or in another part of the house, my mother, quite uninterested in gardening herself, always rushed to call her.

She never had a *fureemu* herself. Nor did she do bonsai. She didn't do most of the things on which she amassed information. Her garden was a profusion of perennials, bulbs, and shrubs, many of which were always threatening to turn into trees. The plantings were indiscriminate. I want to qualify, immediately, "to the superficial eye," but that would not be altogether accurate. In her garden a perpetual contest was staged between order and disorder. She had her own tastes, of course, but they were catholic, accommodating limitations on the part of both seller and buyer. There were grand stores whose names she invoked from the memory of prewar affluence but rarely visited; most of her purchases came from shrine and temple fairs, especially the two near our house, as her ambit shrank. My own favorite were the spring fairs where we picked up more small pots than we could carry and staggered home, the physical struggle mitigating greedy expenditure and allowing for deep contentment. Some years, on April 8, the Buddha's birthday, we made more than one trip to the temple fair. That was before the funeral hall was built and more and more of the grounds given over to the remunerative activities associated with death.

My grandmother planted the yield from those expeditions where she could. For the most part the newcomers were small enough and her knowledge of her garden so intimate that space was found where no other eye could see it. On occasion her purchases were not so modest. She had, characteristically unbeknownst to any of us, yearned for a hawthorn bush for years. When one appeared at our local shrine fair, she hesitated, went back twice, and finally brought it home.

There was even a brief period when my mother and grandmother went on hikes and returned triumphantly with plastic bags filled with rooted wildflowers. Their identities confirmed in botanical dictionaries, they were carefully transplanted in the most favorable spots.

The garden changed over time. The earliest version I think of as the postwar garden. Only two or three trees, then an array of annuals and perennials providing homely color: hollyhocks, gladiolas, sweet williams, cosmos, straw flowers, snapdragons, phlox, primroses. These were commonplace then, but they disappeared from Tokyo in the course of economic recovery. Soaring land prices produced ever more minute plots, and towering structures shut out the light needed by plants hungry for sun and space. As they became harder to grow, they obligingly became unfashionable. (In the farms of the metropolitan prefectures, however, I found the postwar garden flourishing into the 1980s: spindly hollyhocks and spidery cosmos brightening the edges of family plots.)

My grandmother's garden changed too as the neighbors' houses grew taller and the saplings bought by one or another aunt according to the rhythm of their disposable income grew into trees. In the late 1960s, when my grandparents rebuilt their house, they also demolished the air-raid shelter—the Mountain of our childhood—in their garden. The rhododendrons, azaleas, and flowering quince, once set in the ground, expanded in girth and height as if to make up for lost time. The hydrangea got squeezed in between the rhododendron and an azalea that had stopped blooming. My grandmother's middle daughter, the one who moved to Nagasaki, had her planting more than half a dozen camellias. Their leaves— good for snail removal, as I was to discover—spread their dark glow throughout the garden and altered the balance of light and shadow.

Half the camellias came when my aunt moved because she did not want them to fall into the hands of strangers. My grandmother took in her daughters' cast-off or ailing plants as if they were stray animals and made room for all without regard for her own taste. In this way, too, her garden ran out of space and light for postwar and other kinds of flowers. Just as well, too, for she ran out of money with which to indulge even her modest whims. The camellia-loving daughter began to send her seed catalogues just for the illustrations, which she pored over with delight.

She continued to care for every shrub, tree, and plant she had caused to be rooted, inspecting, pruning, spraying, sweeping from a maze of paths known only to her. She grew oddly fanatical about weeding, resorting to magnifying glass and tweezers in order to extract the most hateful intruders in their spring infancy. In her early eighties she was still wielding pruning shears, attached to a pole the length of her body, so as to provide a modicum of light for the low-growing ones of her domain. She said pruning kept her shoulders from stiffening. And she still pumped the squeaky well for watering. This was when she had begun to prefer light sweaters even in the heart of winter because the bulky ones weighed so on her shoulders. Still, it was all that my mother could do to keep her from going out before six in the morning.

What did my grandmother find in her garden, in flowers and trees everywhere, on the roadside, in books, on the television screen? She never grew anything edible except during the acute food shortage immediately after the war, and even then it was just a bit of tomato and corn. My mother, seeing the achingly tender green of persimmon leaves in spring, would exclaim, Don't they look delicious? Couldn't we use them in tempura? At which my grandmother would laugh, and I would pipe up with the saying, Dumplings over flowers.

I'm sure my grandmother spent the happiest years of her life in her garden. There are likely explanations for this: the wordless vitality of the plant kingdom, the relief of work in the open air, the tactile pleasure of soil. Not to mention beauty, or escape from the brutal or merely chattering demand of family. But listing these doesn't bring me closer to grasping that attachment, or more likely obsession. And perhaps I should amend "happiest" to "most intense," if by that is meant absence of the extraneous, the absence of separation from moment and task: I seem to recall her saying, In the garden I don't think about anything.

· · ·

She was not given to abstraction. She was not, really, much inclined to speech on any subject. I have almost no understanding of her relationship to reading. In my girlhood I knew her as an avid reader of foreign detective fiction and newspapers—three dailies, morning and evening editions, read front to back in her heyday. In my adulthood she was mostly just a newspaper reader, whether because television took up more of her so-called leisure or because she simply had less wakeful leisure. When she wanted something more, it was the essayists she read as a young woman. She didn't care for fiction, she said, and she especially didn't care for contemporary fiction writers. Anyway, they couldn't compare with the old masters like Tanizaki, let alone Sōseki. If pressed as to why they were great she would say, They knew so many Chinese characters.

It's never been possible for me to think of my grandmother as silly or stupid. But that answer seemed so absurd that, lacking imagination but full of presumptions about creativity and meaning, I dismissed it. But what did she mean then? And why or how was she also the person who suggested that I read the essays of Bruno Taut on Japanese architecture?

I never thought to ask. I simply took, without question, her love—there turns out to be no other English word that will do—for me and mine in all the forms it expressed itself.

I counted on her to take care of me, no matter how old I was—and, more to the point, no matter how old she was. And so she did, until her stroke.

I'll never know the answers to the questions I didn't ask her. They might have been nonsense questions. My grandmother and I loved each other unconditionally; I didn't think to understand it when I was four, and I didn't need to at forty. Only now, on the threshold of absolute parting, do I appreciate as privilege the absence of the compulsion to understand.

.   .   .

"My life closed twice before its close." An English exam in the tenth grade asked me to puzzle out that line from Dickinson.

Decades of anticipatory dread coalesced in that instant when my aunt next door called with the news of the stroke.

There died the fantasy, twin of dread, that I would—not—in the end, make her life come out right.

She went into a coma after that.

By the time I made the slow flight over the Pacific and arrived at her bedside, she was breathing noisily through open, cracked lips. The room was busy. Nurses worked on one part or another of her body; young doctors marched in and out. How she would have hated being the center of attention, I thought, although it was really no longer "she" who attracted it but an ensemble of biochemical signs.

I crouched over her head for a long time, holding her free wrist, calling to her, telling her who I was. The worst of it was that I couldn't believe in it. My parting had already taken place, voicelessly, on the other side of the Pacific, and now, painfully, comically, I was enacting a scene learned from movies and television.

But I could not not do it.

Be careful what you say, the nurses said, both in warning and encouragement. Patients in coma can hear even if they can't answer.

So I crouched and called.

My attention had slackened by the time my grandmother began turning her head, so slowly that it was scarcely perceptible. It was her open eyes that startled me. She fixed her gaze on my face. Her face was expressionless, or if anything stern, the way a face that has only been turned to us in affection looks when it is suddenly emptied of that history.

As she continued to gaze, unblinking, the sternness softened to bewilderment, and then to grave sorrow. I lost track of the bustle in the room. She stared, and I waited.

And sometime during that long moment, the tears formed and began coursing down her cheek.

· · ·

Since then, we've had several partings and several reunions, though none as momentous as that. Habituation to separation by the Pacific—and most hatefully, busyness—rationalizes the capacity for sorrow even in the shadow of death.

For my mother, everyday minutes have ticked on quietly, shaken by occasional bouts of fever, convulsion, and heart-stopping ambulance trips to the hospital. Each recovery is as precious as the first. Or rather, the fact of recovery grows more precious as its extent diminishes. Sometimes my mother leans over and rests her cheek against her mother's in grieving joy. She does not do this in the presence of her sisters.

My mother is the first-born child. She herself is looking more and more frail. She is embarking on her eighth decade of life. Seventy is no longer old in Japan or most safe parts of the world. But my mother is arriving at seventy after four years of demands comparable to those faced by young parents of infants. She has not slept through the night, for instance. For her, there is no relief to look forward to. That she would *want* to look forward to, that is.

My mother's oeuvre will have been the care of her mother. Girlhood exhausted in wartime, young womanhood in a marriage joyless at best and humiliating at worst, yielding a single child living half a world away. . . . Through it all her mother sheltered her, appreciated her labor—including the management of my grandfather—submitted to her scoldings, chuckled over her clumsiness, and shared in her enthusiasms for James Dean, college and professional baseball (Waseda and Taiyō Whales, now the Yokohama Baystars), sumo (Tochinishiki), detective fiction (American, English, and continental), socialist politics, and pleasures and worries about grandchildren and great-grandchildren as they appeared.

It's as if all of that had coalesced into days and nights of devotion during the past four years. And perhaps that is what is corrosive to her sisters, for it seems to enact, again, their own comparative distance from their mother.

To say that my mother's care of her mother, my grandmother, will have been her oeuvre doesn't allow me to shed my own bad faith. For I've been too busy, too much a person with worldly engagements, to prevent the development of this oeuvre. I know this doesn't particularly distinguish me, that most people my age in my part of the world, women as well as men, aren't free to help their family members through a slow, noninstitutional dying.

On the other hand, to suggest that it's only a combination of historical accident and personal misfortune that has *allowed* my mother to care for her mother doesn't do justice to her timid, invincible character—her genius of temperament.

· · ·

Her mother is my mother's jewel, whose luster grows as her daughter fades.

ONE YEAR LATER

The pleasurable anticipation of a birthday up until the age of twelve or thirteen had to do not only with the presents but with the miracle of how tonight I was only nine, but tomorrow morning I would be ten. When my mother turned seventy, she lost confidence, overnight, about her ability to care for her mother.

Even though her sisters had begun to help, my mother's spirit had been broken by the accumulation of worries past and anticipated. Her announcement took the form of the question, How can I bear having to call the ambulance again?

· · ·

Suminareta is a participle literally meaning "having inhabited and therefore grown habituated to." I read into it bidirectional process, not just static condition, of the act of residence transforming both place and person.

My grandmother moaned on the stretcher taking her from her *suminareta* home to a hospital for the elderly.

.   .   .

Her younger sister, my Auntie with colon cancer, died in May, well before another long hard summer set in. During her last days, she called for her sister more often than for her own daughters, reported the eldest. This cousin gave me her mother's fan. It is a fabric fan, with dark butterflies against a translucent navy blue ground. The wood has been dyed to match, and the fan opens with the ease of frequent use.

I never saw Auntie again after our reunion. Her fan joins that summer to the ones unfolding before me.

.   .   .

By autumn of that anniversary year, with the milestones of the end of the war—Hiroshima, Nagasaki, August 15— safely passed, it looked as if the last chapter of postwar history had been just about written. Then Okinawa erupted with the rape of a schoolgirl by U.S. servicemen. The extraordinary mobilizing power of that incident disappointed and confused me: if people—adults—really minded the disproportionate presence of U.S. troops and the Japanese government that kept them there, why did it take the rape of a child to make their anger visible? And why wasn't there a general now-we-get-it response to the cause of the former military comfort women, many of whom had been not much older than the Okinawan girl? What will make it possible for societies to acknowledge crimes against women as crimes without tacitly overvaluing, almost nationalizing, female chastity? Watching the coverage from the American side of the Pacific, it was impossible to ignore the suffering of the families of the perpetrators—the race and class dimensions, therefore, of the American military presence paid for so substantially by the Japanese government.

Of course, I knew there were Okinawans and other Japanese who had worked on some of these issues for a long time. But I also knew how hard it was, after the emotional and principled objections to the military had been raised, to think through the knot of its huge role in the Okinawan economy. Okinawa has been distinctly poorer than other parts of Japan, but it's Japanese enough for its tropical fruits to be too expensive for the export market. It bothered me that the rape of a schoolgirl seemed to allow people to jump past the slow, hard questions.

Now I'm embarrassed to think of how long it took me to remember that the spark of history isn't usually a matter of choice.

·   ·   ·

I still mull over that spark. And it's not clear what will emerge now that the flames have subsided. But at least for a moment, many Japanese awoke for the first time in a quarter-century to the actuality of the U.S.-Japan security system, fattening since the cold war under cover of bureaucratic management. And together with continuing controversy over the government-sponsored but not government-funded "compensation" to former military comfort women, the Okinawan challenge— and no doubt the new popularity of Okinawan music—may, for a moment, feed the impulse to reexamine wartime and post-war history as well as the conditions of democracy in Japan.

.   .   .

As Governor Ota of Okinawa relinquishes his battle with the central government and receives promises of economic revital-ization in return, I can't help hoping that people will put next to the statistic about Okinawa having the lowest per capita in-come the statistic that Japanese live longest there. And then go on to think about the relation of peace and security issues to the problems of aging, of nuclear power, of chronic bullying in schools. It is dizzying, the chain of things to care about. The triumph in having one municipality or another reject a new reactor might be muted should it mean stepped-up ex-port of "safe Japanese reactors" to more economically vul-nerable neighbors in southeast Asia. The specter of discrimination, unleashed by the outbreak of 0157 (*E. coli*), among schoolchildren, within businesses, between regions af-flicted and those apparently safe, should remind us of how sci-entific knowledge—about how disease is transmitted, for example—crumbles before perceived threats to livelihood. And we might hesitate before consigning the Great Awaji-Hanshin Earthquake to history by juxtaposing the dazzle of reconstruction with the persistence of suicide among survivors.

.   .   .

There it is again, the tired voice, pedagogical and, worse, un-believing. What about that energy released at the time of the earthquake, in everybody who took to the road, on bicycle and foot, carrying water and rice balls, who went on to build tent villages, who found themselves spellbound by the details of life before the unexpected appearance of death? And that passion for mutuality in those college students said to be apolitical and consumption-besotted who encircled the Health Ministry on behalf of one of their own, a hemophiliac who became HIV-positive through contaminated blood? (Their actions surely helped generate an unexpected flood of volunteers, by no means all young, for the first international AIDS conference to be hosted in Japan.)

Imagine the energy in the hunger for meaning coiled just beneath the indifference of routine. It mustn't be left for the Education Ministry to capture by mandating volunteer activities as a condition for school advancement.

. . .

And of course alienation from such hunger isn't a condition restricted to young people, in Japan and elsewhere.

The hunger for meaning is also a hunger for experience. As soon as I write these words, I know, with a weariness that itself verges on indifference, that I will seem to be and no doubt am in the realm of nostalgia. Will its low glow point us to the future? Its bittersweet warmth stir our innards and set us trudging? Lazily and sadly, I imagine that only catastrophe can disrupt the condition I nevertheless persist in calling alienation. It comes in many shapes and intensities, alienation does, depending on where and when you live. The particular incarnation I'm thinking of is the dull twin of sleek and speedy prosperity.

But how to shake off this lassitude? It's at once lonely and deindividuating, damaging for persons and for society. If nostalgia is useful, it must be so as a tool of history, as kindling for a common future.

. . .

I never saw my grandma with the kitty sitting on her bench. In fact, there were no signs of her kitty at all. But I would run into her walking, even quite far from home, or sweeping the street around her house, picking up the recalcitrant leaves with her fingers. One night, taking a stroll with my children in her neighborhood, I heard an ambulance screeching by. We chased it until it halted, heartstoppingly near her house. Then we sighed and walked on, guilty in our relief, knowing that a cycle of trauma, anxiety, and long months or even years of care could be unfolding for someone else.

. . .

Sometimes, when I think of my grandmother in her hospital bed, I'm crushed by our lopsided exchange of care and affection. She cared, and I received. Then the memory of the weight of her body in my arms comes to me as consolation, and more. That memory has the weight of what she never put into words. My arms bear, for now, the memory of the history stored in her body.

I'll never forget the empty bed after she was taken to the hospital. Her room was unanchored. I had been stupid about the power of simple presence.

From My Grandmother's Bedside

Whenever I address a postcard to my mother, just beginning to try on the designation of "senior citizen," I find a tactile pleasure in writing the characters of her name. A person lives, for now, who answers to that name to receive my message.

Obaachama as young wife and mother

NOTES

p. vii   *"Walking-Stick Pass"* "Tsuetsuki Tōge," in Ishigaki's *Yūmoa no sakoku* (The Isolated Land of Humor) (Tokyo: Chikuma Shobō, 1987), 250–51. Translation published with permission of the author. Other versions of this poem, along with several other Ishigaki poems, may be found in Kenneth Rexroth and Ikuko Atsumi, trans., *Women Poets of Japan* (New York: New Directions, 1977), 97–98, and Sato Hiroaki and Burton Watson, eds. and trans., *From the Country of Eight Islands: An Anthology of Japanese Poetry* (N.Y.: Anchor Books, 1981), 575. I take this opportunity to thank Yukie Ohta and Rie Takagi for the pleasure of discussing Ishigaki's poetry as they prepared their translations of several selections, published in *positions east asia cultures critique* 3, no. 3 (Winter 1995): 723–27.

p. xi   *"Steamboat"* The poem "Kisen" may be found with Ishigaki's commentary in her *Shi no naka no fūkei—kurashi no naka ni yomigaeru* (The Landscape of Poems—Quickening in Everyday Life) (Tokyo: Shufu no Tomosha, 1992), 104–5.

p. xiv   *"It is not"* The first passage comes from "Seikatsu no naka no shi" (Poetry in Everyday Life) in *Yūmoa no sakoku*, 160. The second is from "Seikatsu to shi" (Everyday Life and Poetry), 288, from the same collection of essays. A handy selection of Ishigaki's poems is *Ishigaki Rin shishū* (Ishigaki Rin Poetry Collection), Gendai shi bunko (Library of Modern Poetry), vol. 46 (Tokyo: Shichōsha, 1971).

Notes

p. 13   *Ishigaki Rin* I can no longer find this passage. Shamelessly, I asked Ms. Ishigaki. She reread her own two volumes in one of which I am certain it appears, *Yumoa no sakoku* and *Honoo ni te o kazashite* (Tokyo: Chikuma Shobō, 1992), and could not find it either. I remain convinced it is a fugitive passage, not an invented one.

p. 54   *In the news* Press reports from 18 July 1995 and a few days thereafter.

p. 60   *Hiroshima series* Domon Ken, *Dokyumento Nihon [1935–1967]* (Document Japan), vol. 4 of *Domon Ken no Showa* (Domon Ken's Showa), ed. Daiichi Āto Centā (5 vols., Tokyo: Shogakukan, 1995), 109 (no. 319).

p. 60   *Chikuhō coal mine* "Bentō o mottenai ko" (Child without a Lunch) in *Dokyumento Nihon*, 122 (no. 341).

p. 61   *It is my view* "Demo shuzai to koji junrei" (On Covering Demonstrations and Pilgrimages to Ancient Temples), *Asahi Shimbun*, 11 March 1968, cited in *Koji junrei: Domon Ken-ten* (Pilgrimages to Ancient Temples: A Domon Ken Exhibit), ed. Takeuchi Keiko and Mainichi Shimbunsha Kikaku Jigyōbu (Tokyo: Mainichi Shimbunsha, 1995), 92.

p. 65   *breathtaking shots* *Dokyumento Nihon* 9 (no. 8); 7 (no. 5); 26 (no. 68).

p. 66   *inductees* *Dokyumento Nihon*, 24–29.

p. 66   *nurses in training* Ibid., 33–35.

p. 67   *farm women* Ibid., 42 (no. 117).

p. 69   *send-off party* No. 14 (February, 1938), reproduced in *Dokyumento Nihon*, 30 (no. 83).

p. 71   *photo of him judging* Domon Ken, *Shashin hihyō* (Photo Criticisms) (Tokyo: Daviddosha, 1974).

p. 79   *teachers recall* *Tokyo Shimbun*, 21 August 1995, 20.

p. 88   *Ishigaki Rin* "Onna no teshigoto" (Women's Handwork) in *Honoo ni te o kazashite*, 50–53.

p. 97   *A citizens' group* "Genbaku tōka de Kankoku wa dokuritsu" (With Atomic Bombing, Korean Independence), *Tokyo Shimbun*, 26 July 1995, 3.

p. 98   *This debate* Recent representatives of these two positions are Gar

Notes

Alperovitz, *The Decision to Use the Atomic Bomb and the Architecture of an American Myth* (N.Y.: Alfred A. Knopf, 1995) and Murray Sayle, "Letter from Hiroshima: Did the Bomb End the War?" *The New Yorker* (31 July 1995), 40–64.

p. 101   *Marshall Islands*   Kunda Dixit, "Marshall Islands—Environment: South Pacific's Lone Nuclear Voice," Inter Press Service, 3 July 1995; "Marshall Islands Give Go Ahead for Nuclear Waste Dump Study," Deutsche Presse-Agentur, 10 May 1995; "Nihon no kaku gomi, waga mujintō e" (Bring Japanese Nuclear Wastes to Our Uninhabited Islands), *Asahi Shimbun*, 3 November 1996, 1.

p. 102   *all-night talk show* "Asa made nama terebi" (Live TV till Morning), TV Asahi (12 August 1995: midnight–6:00 A.M.).

p. 108   *United Steel Workers* "Enora Gei o mō ichido" (The *Enola Gay* Once More), *Tokyo Shimbun* (evening edition) 18 July 1995, 9; "Rōdō funsō ga kageki demo ni; 'Enora Gei o mō ichido' o kakageru" (Labor Dispute Leads to Extremist Demonstration; Proclaims "*The Enola Gay* Once More"), *Asahi Shimbun*, 19 July 1995, 14. Since I could not find coverage of this event in the American press, I can only guess what the (presumably) English original was from the Japanese translation.

p. 122   *The first play* The play is *Yoshinobu inochigoi* (Begging for Yoshinobu's Life) by Mayama Seika.

p. 130   *Ueno Zoo* "Omoikkiri terebi" (TV All the Way), NTV (11 August 1995, noon–1:55 P.M.).

p. 131   *Domon Ken* "Yakiimo dorobō" (Sweet Potato Thief), *Dokyumento Nihon*, 57 (no. 162).

p. 139   *art songs* The songs mentioned here may be found in standard Japanese songbooks, such as *Nihon Meika 110 kyokushū / 110 Japanese Famous Songs*, vol. 2 (Tokyo: Zen-on Music Co., Ltd., 1966).

p. 157   *one mother . . . Some mothers* "Mōningu EYE" (Morning Eye), TBS (15 August 1995, 8:30–10:00 A.M.).

p. 158   *Tokkō pilot* Ibid.

Notes

p. 159   *Unit 8406* "Sengo 5onen tokubetsu kikaku: Nihon no han-seiki—wareware wa nani o ushinatta no ka" (Special Program on the Fiftieth Year after the War: Our Half-Century—What Is It That We Lost?), Terebi Tokyo (13 August 1995, 2:00–4:00 P.M.).

p. 159   *Unit 731* "Watakushi wa 731 Butaiin datta: jintai jikken 5onenme no kokuhaku" (I Was a Member of Unit 731: A Confession of the Fiftieth Year after Human Experimentation), NHK 1 (4 August 1995, 8:35–9:30 A.M.).

p. 160   *Japan Air Lines* "Nikkōki tsuiraku kara 10nen" (The JAL Crash Ten Years Later), TV Asahi (12 August 1995, 5:30–6:00 P.M.).

p. 166   *Gar Alperovitz The Decision to Use the Atomic Bomb*, 613.

p. 170   *"When I was"* "Watashi ga ichiban kireidatta toki" (1958), set to music, as it turns out, by Pete Seeger. See his charming discussion along with the music and even the Japanese text in Pete Seeger, *Where Have All the Flowers Gone: A Singer's Stories, Songs, Seeds, Robberies*, ed. Peter Blood (Bethlehem, Pa.: Sing-Out Corporation: 1993), 96–98. A translation of this and several other poems by Ibaragi, as well as others by Ishigaki Rin, are to be found in Leza Lowitz and Miyuki Aoyama, eds. and trans., *Other Side River* (Berkeley, Calif.: Stone Bridge Press, 1995). Other samples of Ishigaki and Ibaragi may be found in Kijima Hajime, ed., *The Poetry of Postwar Japan* (Iowa City: University of Iowa Press, 1975); James Kirkup, trans., and A. R. Davis, ed., *Modern Japanese Poetry* (Queensland, Australia: University of Queensland Press, 1978); and Rexroth and Atsumi, *Japanese Women Poets. When I Was at My Most Beautiful and Other Poems, 1953–1982*, translated by Peter Robinson and Fumiko Horikawa (Cambridge, Eng.: Skate Press, 1992), is a sampler of Ibaragi's poetry.

p. 175   *W. S. Merwin* "For the Anniversary of My Death," from the collection *The Lice* (1967), in W. S. Merwin, *Selected Poems* (New York: Atheneum, 1988), 133.

p. 181   *"Mother"* "Okaasan" from *Utsukushii wakare no asa* (The Morning of the Beautiful Farewell), lyrics by Sakata Hiroo and music by Nakada Yoshinao (Tokyo: Kawai Shuppan, 1974).

Designer:	Steve Renick
Compositor:	Publication Services, Inc.
Text:	11/15 Centaur
Display:	Bernhard
Printer:	Haddon Craftsmen
Binder:	Haddon Craftsmen